PROFESSOR PUGWASH
THE MAN WHO FOUGHT NUKES

The Life of
Sir Joseph Rotblat

Kit Hill

ryelands

Front cover photograph: *Joseph Rotblat attending the 1957 conference at Pugwash, Nova Scotia.*

Back cover photograph:
Sir Joseph Rotblat with the Vice-Chancellor, Professor Drummond Bone at the opening of the Rotblat Lecture Theatre, University of Liverpool, 9 April 2003. Courtesy, University of Liverpool, Corporate Communications

Originally published by Halsgrove
under the Ryelands imprint, 2008

British Library Cataloguing-in-Publication Data
A CIP record for this title is available from the British Library

ISBN 978 1 906551 04 9

RYELANDS
Halsgrove House
Ryelands Industrial Estate
Bagley Road, Wellington, Somerset TA21 9PZ
Tel: 01823 653777   Fax: 01823 216796
email: sales@halsgrove.com
website: www.halsgrove.com

Printed in Great Britain by Short Run Press, Exeter

CONTENTS

The Author. Courtesy World Health Organization (1960)

FOREWORD

By Lord Rees, Astronomer Royal and President of the Royal Society

I am delighted that this book, by a longstanding colleague of Jo Rotblat in UK Pugwash, will bring knowledge of this great man to a wider readership, and hopefully inspire many of the younger generation by his example.

The attitudes of my generation were moulded by the early CND marches and the Cuba crisis. I read Bertrand Russell's essays, and the text of his BBC lectures on "Man's Peril". I later learnt of the historic Russell-Einstein declaration, whose authors wrote that they were "speaking on this occasion not as members of this or that nation, continent or creed, but as human beings, members of the species Man, whose continued existence is in doubt". I learnt only later that the impetus for this manifesto came from Jo Rotblat. Nor could I foresee that I would have the privilege, from the 1980s onwards, of participating in Pugwash activities with this astonishing man. Jo Rotblat helped to make the first atomic bomb. But, for decades thereafter, he campaigned to control the powers he had helped to unleash. Until the last months of his long life he pursued this aim with the dynamism of a man half his age, inspiring many others to join the cause. Even in his 90s he could still captivate student audiences – inspiring them as he had earlier inspired so many of us.

In the 1960s and '70s, the superpowers could have stumbled towards Armageddon through muddle and miscalculation. Jo advocated ridding the world entirely of nuclear weapons. This view was widely derided as woolly idealism. But it gained broader "establishment" support over the years. Indeed, the 1977 Canberra Commission – on which Jo sat, along with among its members many distinguished international politicians and ex-military figures – put forward step-by-step proposals for eliminating nuclear weapons completely. Its report stated that "The proposition that nuclear weapons can be retained in perpetuity and never used – accidentally or by decision – defies credibility." Among those on the Canberra Commission was Robert McNamara. As US Secretary of Defense in the 1960s, McNamara was in charge of the US nuclear arsenal at the time of the Cuba missile standoff. He later wrote that this was the most dangerous moment in history: "We came within a hairbreadth of nuclear war without realising it. It's no credit to us that we escaped – Krushchev and Kennedy were lucky as well as wise".

The nuclear threat is based on basic science that dates from the 1930s, when Jo Rotblat was a young researcher. The spin-offs from 21st-century science offer immense hope, and exciting prospects. But they also, like nuclear science, may have a downside. Small sub-national groups can be empowered by new kinds of weapons that are easier to develop and far harder to monitor than nuclear weapons. The collective impacts of humankind on the biosphere, climate and oceans are unprecedented. These environmentally driven threats – "threats without enemies" – should loom as large in the political perspective as did the East/West political divide during the Cold War era.

Jo Rotblat favoured a "Hippocratic Oath", whereby scientists would pledge themselves to use their talents to human benefit. Whether or not such an oath would have substance, scientists surely have a special responsibility. It is their ideas that form the basis of new technology. The post-World War II nuclear scientists set us a fine example. They did not say that they were "just scientists" and that the use made of their work was up to politicians: they took the line that all scientists should retain a concern with how their ideas are applied.

The challenges of the 21st century are more complex and intractable than those of the nuclear age. Wise choices will require idealistic and effective campaigners – not just physicists, but biologists, computer experts and environmentalists as well: latter-day counterparts of Jo Rotblat, inspired by his vision, and building on his legacy.

Martin Rees

PREFACE

In a thousand years' time, if anyone is still around, historians will identify the 20th century as the era when people not only killed each other off in larger numbers than ever before, but then discovered the means for destroying their entire civilisation. Joseph Rotblat lived through almost all of that century and found himself, quite accidentally, at the very centre of this discovery, with all the huge responsibility that it involved.

He was born in Poland, where he lived through the terrible upheavals of the 1914-18 war. By the time he was thirty he had become a world-class physicist, finding himself working on some of the most exciting scientific developments of the century. With the onset of World War II this led him to the centre of work, first in Britain and then the USA, on the nuclear bomb. When he learned that the justification for the project had secretly been changed, he resigned in protest and went on to lead a world-wide movement for abolishing nuclear weapons, eventually being awarded a Nobel Peace Prize for his work. Ever a warm, humane and congenial person, his remarkable story thus involves many aspects of the history, people, politics and science of the 20th century.

In Rotblat's life and work he interacted with many other interesting people, some of them quite famous, from many walks of life. It has only been possible to bring a small number of these into the tale, several of them chosen because they were people whom I too had known. Joseph Rotblat was a man of wide-ranging interests and talent, but central to his life story were the developments that were taking place during his lifetime of our understanding of the basic nature of matter – nuclear physics – and the opportunities for practical application to which this led. It is a sad reflection on our modern culture that many people turn away in fright at the suggestion that they might try to understand a little physics. It is with just such people in mind that I have designed this book. Two of the things that

I have done are, firstly, to put most of the even slightly technical stuff in to "boxes", thus avoiding interruption to the main story; and second, even in the boxes, to try to talk common sense. (Serious physicists will wince when they find me likening an atom to a set of kitchen shelves.) Don't be frightened.

Just a few incidents need to be read with tongue in cheek – the bits about the orchard, and the climb to Morskie Oko for example – but, even though some of the rest may be hard to believe, it is quite true.

This is a complex story and, in trying to make it a good read for different backgrounds and ages, and to get the facts right, I have asked for honest comments from a variety of people of different ages and experience. Thanks for this to: Beth Backhouse and friends, Freddy and Sally Milne, Sandra Butcher, Catherine Hill, Jack Harris and Halina Sand.

Finally, what about the funny name? For most people, in Britain at least, the word Pugwash rings a nautical bell. Captain Horatio Pugwash first made a public appearance, in 1950, as a cartoon character in the first issue of a new children's comic, the Eagle. Its publishers had high ambitions and circulated copies of that issue to heads of all the Oxford and Cambridge colleges – in the apparent hope that their students would become avid readers. Perhaps as a result the Captain's career progressed well and – to paraphrase WS Gilbert –

> He entertained the public so successfully
> That he got himself promoted to the new TV.

His first performance there (initially in black and white) was on 22 October 1957, just a few weeks after our Professor's first public appearance at Pugwash, Nova Scotia. But how the Eagle originally chose for their cartoon the name of that remote Canadian fishing village still remains a mystery.

Kit Hill, 2008

JÓZIO

The 5th of August was one of the hottest days of the summer. Very close, without a breath of wind; the heavy clouds piling up on the horizon suggested a coming storm. That might cool things down a bit but, even so, it would still be hours away.

Apart from the happy chatter of the children, who were building a camp in the shade of one of the old apple trees, there was not much to disturb the peace of the orchard – just the rumble of an occasional horse-drawn cart in the cobbled street beyond the house, and the cackle of a neighbour's hen, telling the world of the arrival of her latest egg. Even the blackbird had gone silent – too exhausted to bother making a meal of one of the early windfall apples.

And then there was a call: "Józio, Motek, Eva – Come inside – Quickly!"

From the tone of their mother's voice they realised that she was serious. It was no good pretending that they hadn't heard. A pity, because the camp was starting to look rather good - Jòzio had been doing a clever job of making things out of bits and pieces.

"Come in, and shut the door"

It wasn't long since lunch, but Dad was already home. He had a business supplying paper to printers and people like that, all over Warsaw, and he would usually be out until late working at his warehouse, or perhaps making a delivery with one of his horse-drawn vans. He was a kindly person, and a good father, but today he was looking unusually worried, and Mum was looking very serious too – standing by the front window, and anxiously glancing out.

"Why do we have to come in, Mum? We haven't finished making our camp".

She looked at Dad. "You had better tell them Zelman".

"Did you hear any strange noises, children, when you were building your camp?"

"Well – yes. There was thunder. At least it was a bit like thunder, but more like the guns that the soldiers fire from the castle on St Casimir's Day".

"I am afraid you are right. It is guns. But it is not Polish guns. There is a war, and the German army is coming towards Warsaw. I was told just now that they are only a few kilometres away."

All this happened in 1915, when Józio was nearly seven. He was one of the lucky ones – part of a large, noisy and happy family, who were able to have a big house and garden, a pet pony, plenty to eat, and exciting trips in the summer holidays – a great deal more than most people in Warsaw at that time.

The family – the Rotblats – spoke Polish and thought of themselves as Polish. But this was very odd because, for the past 50 years, there hadn't been a country called Poland – it had been swallowed up by Russia. The problem was that Poland had always found itself squeezed between three powerful neighbours: Russia to the East, Prussia to the West, and Austria-Hungary to the South, with the Baltic Sea on the north. For a thousand years it had grown, shrunk, and grown again, forever moving its borders. It had once extended out to Moscow and beyond in the east. But now it had disappeared altogether, and the Russians had even made it illegal for Polish to be spoken in schools. Once again, the neighbours were picking a fight. This time Germany (which, by then, had absorbed Prussia) had wanted to grab more space. That got them into war, both with Russia on one side and France and Britain on the other. Once again Poland was the pig in the middle.

The war changed everything for Józio's family. All their horses, that were used for hauling the firm's delivery vans, were taken for the war, and so even was the children's pony. Soldiers ransacked the shops, warehouses

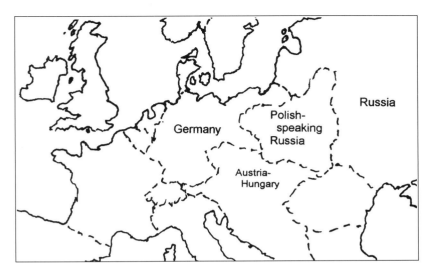

Europe in 1914. Poland only existed as a province of Russia.

and farmers' barns, so that soon there was hardly any food to be found anywhere. Poland in those days had plenty of coal, which was its main form of fuel, but that too disappeared, leaving everyone to freeze in the bitterly cold winters. The family cut down the orchard trees for firewood, and used the space to grow potatoes. But these too froze in the hard winter, often leaving them as their only food as a horrible-tasting rotten mush. Many years later, when he had come to live in England, Józio still couldn't face eating even good, buttered new potatoes, because of the memory that they brought back of that awful wartime diet.

The war went on for another three long years, and then the armies retreated, leaving Poland a free country once again. But things were still in a terrible state – as they were too in Germany and Russia – and it was many years before they recovered. The Rotblat family survived – just – but it was still terribly difficult for them to buy the food and fuel that they needed to keep alive. The family paper business had collapsed during the war and, in a desperate attempt to make some sort of income, they set up, in their basement, an illegal vodka distillery. To supplement this, as soon as he was able, Józio learnt to be an electrician, sometimes finding himself laying cables in weather so cold that his hands couldn't hold a pair of pliers. And then he found that he could earn more by setting up his own electrical repair business. Somehow he found time to visit the library, and to become keen on science fiction. That way he got interested in science, and decided to go off to night school to study physics, hoping to be able to get into university.

The Polish university system in those days was very selective – not academically so much as in who you were and what you could afford. Being Jewish, for instance, was a no-no. For that reason alone Józio would not be able to study at the official University of Warsaw but also, not having properly finished his secondary education, he was not officially qualified. Bad news. Then, one day in 1929, when he had just turned 20, someone told him about an evening institute – the so-called Free University of Poland in Warsaw. He immediately went to find out about it, and was dumbstruck to be told by a lady in the office that the entrance exam was being held the next day. OK – nothing to lose – have a go! But, when he had sat down in the examination room and looked at the paper, his heart sank. Only the second part was about physics – the first was on literature and social history, with impossible questions. His first idea was to get up and leave, but the door was at the far end of the room, and he was too shy and embarrassed to walk out. So he had a go, but was convinced afterwards that he had failed – that was until a week later when the results came out and he was told that he had passed after all. This was fantastic – too good to be true – but one of his teachers told him what had happened. Yes – a lot of the answers that he had written weren't right, but the examiners so liked the way that he had reasoned them that they decided to pass him anyway. This was truly a stroke of luck that made it possible, in the end, for a novice electrician to go on to become world-famous and to win a Nobel Prize.

But that is for the next part of the story. Meanwhile a bit of explanation is needed. We have been talking about "Józio", because that was the family name for him. But he had several other names. His given name, when he was born, was Joseph (written Jósef in Polish), but that was too much of a mouthful for his small niece Frances (Motek's daughter) who decided, and persuaded the rest of the family, that he was now Josh (pronounced Yosh). Then, to his eventual British, and other international colleagues, he universally became Jo.

THE WILY NEUTRON

Chance plays curious tricks. Just down the road from the Rotblat's in Warsaw was the home of the Sklodowskis. In 1867 their daughter Maria had been born there. A very bright girl, she wanted to study chemistry and, as one of the best places to do that was Paris, where her sister, Bronia was already living, that is where she went. Soon she fell in love with one of her teachers, Pierre and, on getting married, took on the name of Marie Sklodowska Curie.

While in Paris she met a physics professor, Henri Becquerel, who had made a very lucky mistake. He had recently heard that a man called Conrad Röntgen, in Germany, had discovered a form of penetrating radiation, and he had the idea that he might be able to produce the same sort of thing if he exposed to sunlight materials that were "fluorescent" (that glowed in the dark). He experimented with several of these materials, exposing them and then putting them on to photographic plates wrapped in black paper. Nothing happened with his first lot of specimens and, by the time he got around to trying his last candidate, that had uranium in it, he had lost the sun – clouds had come up. He had a go, anyhow, hoping that he might get a faint effect from the dim light, but found to his astonishment that the plate had been turned black. He had discovered radioactivity!

As a student project, supervised by Pierre, Marie then set out to do an analysis of a uranium ore called pitchblende, and soon found two new chemical elements that had this property of emitting penetrating radiations. She named the first polonium, after her native country, and the second radium (uranium itself also has this property, but only relatively weakly so).

So, by the time she was 30 she had become world-famous for her part in showing that atoms aren't really "atoms" after all. (The Greek word atom just means "can't be cut".) As it turns out, some kinds of atoms have the habit of suddenly turning into a different kind of atom and, at the same time, shooting out bits and pieces of themselves in all directions. So, such atoms were not really indivisible and Marie described them as "radioactive". The bits and pieces were given names like alpha particles, beta particles and gamma rays.

The Invisible Atom Guessing Game

Democritus' Guess (400 BC)
Everything is made up of "a-toms" - Literally lumps that cannot be cut into smaller pieces. It was not for another 2200 years that people could work out the size of an atom: small enough that there are well over a million million million (10^{18}) of them in a pin-head

Curie's Guess (1898)
Some atoms can have mini-volcanic eruptions – bits and pieces can fly off.

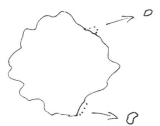

Rutherford's Guess (1911)
An atom is a sort of mini solar system: It seems to have a "nucleus" that is surrounded by a cloud of electrons. The nucleus has a diameter only one ten-thousandth that of the atom, but contains about 99.95% of its mass. (See box: "Common sense …")

"COMMON SENSE" GOES OUT OF THE WINDOW

Rutherford had grown up with a common sense view of the world. Things that you could see and touch behaved according to a reasonable set of rules, which seemed to be good even for astronomy – the movement of the sun and planets for example. Indeed, one of his eminent contemporaries, Lord Kelvin, as recently as 1897, had remarked that there was "nothing more to be discovered in physics". Oh boy! How wrong can you be?

The problem came up when people started to think about the atom. If, as it seemed, the "positively charged" nucleus was surrounded by a cloud of "negatively charged" electrons, how was it that the electrons stayed out there and didn't get attracted down to the nucleus? Perhaps they behave like planets rotating around a star? But that wouldn't do, as they would then rapidly loose energy, slow down, and still crash.

Then, a Danish physicist, Nils Bohr – who had been working with Rutherford, and was good on theoretical thinking – came up with an extraordinary suggestion: forget common sense, what we are dealing with is way smaller than anything we have seen or touched, and maybe there is behaviour there that follows rules that we don't know about. And there were already some curious ideas going around. Bohr knew that, a few years previously, a German called Max Planck had suggested that radiations like visible light and x-rays, instead of being a continuous stream, were made up of little packets of energy, that he called "quanta". And – baffling for the non-physicist – because we have abandoned common sense rules, and our language is based on common sense, it will become impossible clearly to describe what is going on in anything but mathematical language.

In the best that common sense language can do, Bohr's idea was that the atom is somehow like an interconnected set of kitchen shelves, with spaces on each of them for just a small number of each kind of particle – electrons or whatever. Particles get loaded on to the lower shelves first, and need more and more energy to be lifted on to higher shelves. And, if for instance an electron gets lifted up to a very high shelf and then drops down to an empty space in a shelf below, it will give up a packet ("quantum") of energy. Also, if an electron gets pushed so hard that it shoots beyond the top shelf, and into space, the atom has lost a negative charge and so turns positive – in the jargon it has become an "ion", or is "ionised".

Bohr's ideas, which led to what is called "quantum mechanics", were brilliant. They made sense of a whole lot of previously unexplained facts and figures. For instance, the yellow light that you see when you throw salt (sodium chloride) into a fire makes sense if you think that the heat of the fire temporarily lifts electrons in the sodium atom up on to a higher energy level (shelf) and that, when they fall back again, they give up that energy difference as flashes of light. Also (mark of a good theory!) Bohr's ideas made a lot of predictions that could then be tested experimentally. He thought them up, of course, when he was trying to understand the behaviour of atomic electrons, but they eventually helped to unravel the even more complex business of the inner workings of the nucleus. This became critical to interpreting much of Jo Rotblat's experimental discoveries.

This was truly amazing stuff, and it made people start asking all sorts of questions (and trying to guess the answers, which is what science is all about). What were these bits and pieces? What was inside these "atoms"? And what on earth made them decide – sometimes after thousands of years playing dead, but sometimes after only a fraction of a second – to suddenly blow apart?

One of the best, in those days, at the game of "Question and Guess" was a New Zealander, Ernest Rutherford, who had become Professor of Physics at Manchester. It happened that one of the undergraduate students, another Ernest – Ernest Marsden – needed an experimental project. So, under Rutherford's assistant, Hans Geiger (later famous for inventing the Geiger Counter) they put Marsden to work on shooting alpha particles (which are really atoms of helium) at a thin sheet of gold atoms, and measuring the directions they went after collision.

At that time most people thought of atoms as rather like tiny snooker balls. You can easily work out the direction in which a snooker ball will go when it is hit. Maybe Rutherford had a hunch that atoms could be more interesting than snooker balls. In any case, Marsden's alpha particles didn't behave like that. So Rutherford sat down and did the sums. He realised that you could only explain Marsden's results if most of the mass of the atom was concentrated in an even tinier spot at its centre – that he called the "nucleus". This – the idea that an atom has a nucleus surrounded by a

GEIGER COUNTERS AND THINGS

The trouble with atoms is that you can't see them. But, as Becquerel discovered on his photographic plates, radioactive atoms give themselves away when they emit rays and particles. Nowadays there are a lot more ways of detecting these things but two – one that Hans Geiger invented and the other that Ernest Marsden used for his experiments – work well and are still very popular.

A Geiger counter is really very simple. It is a metal tube, a few centimetres in diameter, with a thin wire stretched along its axis. The wire is charged up to a high voltage, but not so high that it starts to spark. However, when a beta particle or gamma ray travels through the gas in the tube, this triggers a small spark, whose electrical charge is fed to a loudspeaker. So, each click-click that you hear tells you that an atom has disintegrated somewhere, and sent its radiation through the counter tube. In the author's photograph, on page 4 of this book, he is shown working with a version of a Geiger counter – a "pulse-ionisation counter" (possibly the world's largest!) – that he had made for identifying natural radioactivity in human tissues

In Ernest Marsden's project he needed to detect alpha particles, which can only penetrate about a twentieth of a millimetre of material – not enough to get through the wall of a Geiger counter. So he used a different trick. When some types of crystal are bombarded by alpha- (or beta-) particles they emit flashes of light. Nowadays these flashes can be picked up by photo-multipliers and turned into electrical pulses, but young Ernest had to do it the hard way. Even the flashes from alpha particles are very faint and so he had to sit for ages, in a darkened room, peering down a microscope that was trained on a screen covered in tiny crystals of lithium fluoride, wait patiently for a flash, and record whereabouts on the screen it occurred.

Dr Geiger's Counter. The window in the top of the counter tube is transparent to beta-particles. When they hit gas molecules inside the tube, they strip off ("negative") electrons, which then rush towards the ("positive") centre wire, causing a spark as they go. The current from each spark makes a click in a loudspeaker, and the meter on the front of the box shows the rate at which the sparks are happening (roughly the "dose-rate").

But you don't need any special kit to be able to see that alpha particles (and therefore radioactive atoms) are around. When an alpha particle hits the surface of a sheet of cellulose nitrate plastic it blasts away a tiny hole which, when the debris has been washed away -"etched"- with acid, is big enough to be seen with a good lens or a slide projector. Using this trick you can, for example, easily measure how much radioactive radon there is in your room.

cloud of electrons – was another mind-blowing breakthrough in guessing how the world is made. All the result of an undergraduate project! (A lot of brilliant discoveries have come from student projects. Perhaps this is because students, unlike their elders and betters, don't think that they know it all and that some things are just "impossible".)

Ernest Marsden working in the author's lab at the Institute of Cancer Research, in 1959 – fifty years after his student project had discovered the atomic nucleus. The instrument that he is working with is for measuring the amount of natural radioactivity that is in our food and our bodies. Brazil nuts and Shredded Wheat are good sources of radium, and there is plenty of polonium in kidneys and green vegetables!

Joseph Rotblat's graduate student card for the University of Warsaw.

But, now back to Józio, aka Jo. He too had shown himself to be a very able undergraduate and, in 1932, became a research student under a Professor Wertenstein, who once had been a research assistant of Marie Curie in Paris.

Like many physicists at that time, Jo and his boss were fascinated by Rutherford's idea of atoms in which a lot of the interesting business seemed to go on in a tiny central nucleus, which itself would sometimes spit out fireworks. What went on inside the nucleus? What was it "made of"?

In the same year that Jo was starting his research, a fellow student of Marsden's from his Manchester time (and good friend of Wertenstein), James Chadwick, was working at Cambridge. He had discovered that one of the bits and pieces of which the nucleus seemed to be made was a particle that, because it was electrically neutral, he called a neutron. So the idea came about that the atomic nucleus might be some sort of plum pudding, with two sorts of plums – yellow and red for instance. The reds were called protons, because they had positive charges that just balanced the negative charges of the swarm of electrons that made up the outer part of the atom.

The job of the yellows, the neutrons, was not too clear, but they seemed to have something to do with the fireworks behaviour. Ordinary carbon atoms, for example, have six protons and six neutrons in their nucleus (thus "carbon 12") and behave as very stable and dull citizens. Add a couple more neutrons however (carbon 14) and the atoms get a bit wobbly, and after an average of some 5500 years, do their fireworks stuff. That is why Ernest Rutherford talked about "wily neutrons": because they are good at sneaking themselves into unexpected places. (To make a long story short, carbon 14 atoms emit beta particles and turn into – stable – nitrogen 14. The carbons 12 and 14 are said to be two different *isotopes* of carbon.)

Meanwhile, back from her wartime ambulance driving, Marie Curie had been busy. Working with her daughter, Irène, they had discovered that, by bombarding them with high-speed charged particles (eg alpha particles), some ordinary, stable atoms could be changed into radioactive atoms: "artificial radioactivity". (This made history in another way. Marie had been the first woman recipient when she and her husband, Pierre, shared a Nobel Prize for their discovery of natural radioactivity, and now she, with Irène, got a second one for their work.)

This too gave Jo ideas and, rather as young Ernest had done, twenty years before, he decided to see if he could learn something from another shooting gallery experiment. This time, he was deliberately shooting at the plum pudding – the nucleus – and using neutrons as bullets. The good thing about neutrons for this job is that, because they don't have an electric charge, they are not repelled by the "positive" charge of the nucleus – as ("positively charged") protons would be, for example.

Jo's first experiments turned out not just to need shooting skills, but con-

Guessing about the Invisible Nucleus

Rutherford's Guess (1911)

The nucleus is a solid lump, with a "positive" electric charge that just balances the total "negative" charges of its surrounding cloud of electrons.

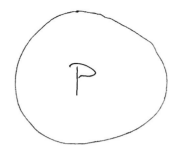

Bohr's Guess (1935)

The nucleus is a sort of plum pudding, containing a number of (positively charged) "protons" and, (apart from in hydrogen), a number of neutral "neutrons". Nuclei of "radioactive" atoms are unstable, and so have the habit of spitting out particles (eg neutrons and alpha particles) until they get stable again.

Rotblat, Hahn, etc's Guess (1939)

Some (particularly very "heavy") nuclei are so unstable that they can split apart ("fission") into two or more smaller atomic nuclei and a number of neutrons. Those neutrons can trigger more fission in nearby nuclei with which they collide.

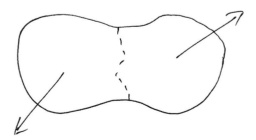

siderable athletic ability as well. Shooting at a silver foil, they had a hunch that the ordinary silver atoms (Silver 107) might pick up a few more neutrons and turn into a different, radioactive, isotope (Silver 110). This turned out to have a "half-life" (the period of time after which half the atoms have decayed away) of only 22 seconds. The problem was that, to test this, the silver foil had to be taken very rapidly to a detector that was far enough away from the neutron source not to be affected by it. Jo was long-legged and athletic and he managed to make the trip, repeated over a hundred times, in seven seconds – all this by dashing down two flights of stairs, through a corridor, through the caretaker's flat, and yet another corridor before reaching the lab. One of the flights of stairs he would take in one jump. It was this that was the downfall (literally) that finally stopped the work – he fell and broke his leg!

But soon they were after shooting bigger stuff. To begin with, gold looked suitable, and it has a big atom. So Wertenstein used his influence to persuade the Polish National Mint to melt down one of their 4kg bars of gold

Otto Hahn was one of the half-dozen physicists, including Rotblat, and also Otto Frisch and Liese Meitner, who between them discovered nuclear fission. Here he is pictured watching as a uranium nucleus is splitting apart to form two nuclei of barium (Ba) and Krypton (Kr), whilst other uranium nuclei and neutrons whizz around in the background.

and mould it to the shape they wanted for their experiments – a cylinder. And then it was arranged that, every morning, Jo would call in at the Mint, pick up the mould (worth around £60,000 today), work with it in the lab and take it back before closing time.

Then they had a better idea – uranium. This looked interesting because such very heavy atoms – and uranium was the heaviest then known - were believed to be already rather unstable. Other experimenters had been finding curious things happening. If you shot neutrons at uranium atoms you could end up finding other sorts of atoms, such as barium and krypton, that were not there before and were about half the weight of uranium. The uranium atoms seemed to have split in two; a process to which they gave a Latin name – *fission*. When Jo followed this up he noticed something else – every time he shot a single neutron at a uranium atom it spewed out several new neutrons; the number of neutrons was being multiplied by the fission process.

Suddenly, what everyone thought was a very geeky and rarified scientific game began to have mind-boggling implications

THINGS FALL APART

Just what was going on in Jo's mind? He knew from his experiments that neutrons were making the uranium atoms break apart and spit out several more neutrons. But there were two more things that he knew from the books. First, that the mass of the uranium atom was greater than the combined mass of the two new atoms that had broken off. (You might well ask how do you weigh atoms. Good question. It can be done, but the answer is for another time.) And secondly, what he also knew was that Albert Einstein had come up with a theory that said that mass can be converted into energy, and *vice versa*. So – might it be that the missing bit of mass when the uranium atom had split apart had changed into energy? (See box: "No Maths …")

Putting all that together he could see that, if more than one of the new neutrons went on to split another uranium atom – and so on, and so on – each time loosing a bit of mass and so releasing a bit of energy, the whole effect could snowball into a huge explosion. And, as if this wasn't enough, people were starting to wonder at that time whether there might be other atoms, apart from uranium that could have this fission behaviour?

Uranium is element no 92, meaning that it had 92 protons in its nucleus, and no-one had yet found traces of anything bigger than that. But, what if there had been other, bigger atoms originally and they had now all decayed away – what would they be like? And could it be possible to re-invent them?

Whilst thinking about this, Jo spotted a scientific paper, written by people working on Ernest Lawrence's cyclotron, in California (see the Cyclotron box, below) that announced the discovery of two new elements, numbers 93 and 94. Jo soon worked out that 94 was likely to behave like uranium, and so might also be able to split apart and trigger an explosion.

NO MATHS PLEASE – WE'RE BRITISH!

Albert Einstein was born in Germany, to a Jewish family who moved round quite a bit and eventually settled in Switzerland, where Albert got a job in the Swiss patent office. It seems to have been a rather boring job, but it gave him a lot of time to think about the maths and physics that he had studied at Zurich technical college. And he started to think that there was something not quite right about what he had been taught. For instance, it was known that light and radio waves travelled in space at about 186 km per second, and that nothing could go faster than that. So what did that mean about things happening at two different places in the universe? When you came to describe the situation in mathematical terms, unlike a small-scale situation in the lab, you found that you had to take into account not just distances in space but also distances in time. And this made him realise that anyone's description of the universe – in which objects are distant in both space and time, and are also moving very fast relative to each other – will be different depending on where they are sitting. In other words, physical behaviour is not cast in stone, but varies relative to how it is observed. This was the basis of Einstein's "Theories of Relativity".

Once you start thinking in this way, and expressing it in mathematical equations, you start to reach some surprising conclusions. One of these was that, as objects travel very fast indeed, approaching the speed of light, their mass appears to increase. Rotblat encountered this phenomenon in his work with cyclotrons: when you want to achieve very high particle energies, and therefore speeds, you find that you have to gradually lower the frequency of the "pushes" to allow for the increase in mass, and therefore inertia. Nice evidence for Einstein's theory!

Another of his startling conclusions was that mass and energy are, in a sense, one and the same thing, and could be converted, one into the other. Once again, it was all bound up with this seemingly "god-given" quantity: the speed of light. To covert a quantity of mass (kilograms) into energy (joules, or watts times seconds) you multiply it by the square of the speed of light:

$$E = mc^2$$

This seemed incredible, but it, too, was confirmed experimentally. In the 1930s a new particle was discovered. It seemed to be an electron, but with a positive charge – so it was dubbed a "positron".

But, the other way in which it differed from an electron was that – a tiny fraction of a second after it had appeared – it vanished in a puff of, well, radiation. From where it disappeared, a couple of gamma rays were emitted, travelling in exactly opposite directions, and with a combined energy (around 1 million electron volts) just equal to the mass equivalent (from the equation) of the disappeared positron. This too came back into Jo's life, later on when he was applying physics in medicine. This vanishing behaviour of positrons turns out to provide a very precise way of locating (for example in the human body) the radioisotope that emitted them in the first place. Nowadays hospital patients are often examined by being given a PET (Positron Emission Tomography) scan.

Now it is time to introduce another character into the story. The Seaborg family had quite a lot in common with the Rotblats. They came from Sweden (which, at one period in its history, had been part of a united kingdom with Poland) and emigrated to America. They had a son who was born just four years after Jo (he had been given the name Glen, but thought it looked better with two n's, so changed it to Glenn). Like the Rotblats in Poland, and of course many others, they went through some quite hard times in the 1920s. At high school Glenn Seaborg particularly liked history and English, but just wasn't interested in science. This was tough, because the rules for going on to college said that he had to take a science class. So, he signed up for the one subject that happened to be offered that year – chemistry. He had struck lucky. His chemistry teacher, Dwight Reid, was one of those people who have charisma, and a real gift and enthusiasm for their job. So, in 1930, Glenn went to college to study chemistry, and nine years later, when Jo was realising the implications of his work, he was working in the world-famous Lawrence Radiation Lab of the University of California.

For physicists, the Lawrence Lab was simply the world's biggest and best shooting gallery. They had built a machine called a cyclotron (see the box) that could accelerate particles like protons to such high speeds that they could smash right in to an atomic nucleus without being deflected by its positive charge. Glenn's job was to do the chemistry to identify the atoms you were left with after such a smash. Doing this, he was able to confirm that the previously non-existent element 94 was indeed, as Jo had predicted, a close cousin of uranium. Some elements had been named after planets – uranium after Uranus, for example, so they called this one plutonium, after Pluto.

Like Jo, it was with pure curiosity to discover how the world works that Glenn and his lab friends had set out to do their experiments. They could not have had any serious idea that they, and a few others like them, were going to change the world forever. But what they had done couldn't be undone – the way things go someone else would have done it soon if they hadn't – and they had to start facing the consequences. Some of the isotopes of plutonium, particularly the 239 one, were indeed fissionable – like uranium – put bluntly, they were bomb material (but also, perhaps, if their behaviour could be controlled, fuel for nuclear electric power generators).

CYCLOTRONS – MAGIC ROUNDABOUTS

We all see electric sparks – for example when someone is connecting up a car battery. It goes too fast to follow by eye, but what is happening is that electrons are being pulled out of the metal in the connector by the electric force (voltage) between it and the other ("positive") connector. The higher the voltage, the more that the electrons are speeded up, or, to put it another way, the more energetic they become. An electron that has travelled from one connector to the other of a 12 volt battery is said to have gained an energy of 12 "electron-volts".

The "beta particles" that were emitted by Marie Curie's radioactive materials – and used by Jo in his first shooting gallery experiments – were also just electrons that had been speeded up by a process inside the nucleus. Some of these had energies up to around a million electron volts (Mev).

But physicists are ambitious people – they always want something better, say 10 Mev, or even 100 Mev. There is a problem, though: it is just about possible to build up an electric force of about a million volts, but then, even with ultra-thick insulation, you can start getting some huge and very nasty sparks. This was the problem that Ernest Lawrence, an American, was thinking about one Saturday morning when he had taken his kids to the play park, and had a bright idea. How about sitting your electron (or even a proton)on a roundabout and, every time that it comes round, giving it a push – something like a thousand volt push – each time making it go faster and faster?

So, he went back to the lab and built a machine to do just that (see diagram). And, because in those days it was fashionable to call every new electronic gizmo a "something-*tron*", he called this a cyclotron (the gadget that drives the kitchen microwave is, similarly, a magnetron).

Cyclotrons soon became a popular tool for physicists but, as they were made bigger and more powerful, a curious problem appeared. As the speed of a particle starts to approach the speed of light, an effect that was predicted by Einstein's theory of relativity starts to make itself felt: the mass of the particle seems to increase. To put it another way, the amount of increase in its speed resulting from a given input of energy (push on the roundabout) decreases. So, in order to get the particles to continue to go faster and faster, you have to synchronise the timing of the pushes to allow for this behaviour. Time for a name-change! It is now called a synchro-cyclotron, and it was one of these that Jo was trying to design and build when he got back to Liverpool, after the war.

Cyclotrons emit charged particles but, if like Jo and Chadwick you want neutrons, you have to use another trick. If, instead of speeding up protons (ions of ordinary hydrogen), you use ions of deuterium ("heavy hydrogen", which has a nucleus made up of one proton and one neutron), and shoot them through a thin sheet of material, some of the protons get knocked out of the nucleus, leaving you with a beam of pure neutrons

The story didn't end there. Physicists went on trying to make bigger and better machines, using the idea behind the cyclotron (push – push – push). One of the latest – the so-called Large Hadron Collider, at a lab called CERN, near Geneva, is about three kilometres in diameter.

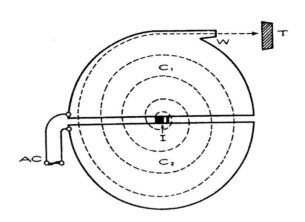

The Cyclotron — a machine for speeding up electrically charged particles by giving them a series of electrical pushes as they travel on a round-about. The particles are fed in to the centre (I) of a pair of D-shaped cavities (C_1 and C_2). An alternating electric voltage (AC) makes the particles move in and out of the two cavities in turn but, as they do so, a magnetic field makes them travel in curved lines, moving faster and faster in a spiral, until they finally shoot out of a thin window (W) and hit a target (T).

The University of Liverpool cyclotron that Jo came to work with in 1939. The roundabout part, in the middle, is surrounded by a powerful electro-magnet and a whole lot of electrical and mechanical gadgetry. This looks rather typical of machines that physicists like to build and work with. This one worked well, and helped make useful discoveries.

A modern, commercially produced machine. Much cleaner and tidier. This one is designed to produce positron-emitting radioisotopes for use in medical "PET" imaging (see the "No Maths Please" box). The isotopes produced by particle bombardment are fed into the Biosynthesizer, where they are chemically incorporated into molecules suitable for tracing biochemical behaviour in the human body.

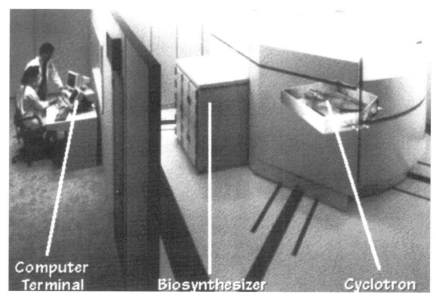

Computer Terminal   Biosynthesizer   Cyclotron

TOLA

Morskie Oko must be one of the most beautiful places in Poland. On the southern border, high up in the Tatra Mountains, it is a deep, clear blue circular lake, almost surrounded by mountains – its name means "eye lake". Jo and his friend Felix Lachman had climbed up there one day in 1930 when they were on a college summer camp in the nearby mountain town of Zakopane. Felix's sister Rachela was at the camp too, with her friend Tola Gryn – they were both studying history and literature. Jo hadn't met Tola before; she was a rather quiet and thoughtful person, tall and dark complexioned. They were both a bit shy, but they seemed just right for each other, and soon became much more than just friends.

Both their families were Jewish and, as we have already seen, in Poland that mattered a lot. In many countries including Poland there was a good deal of bad feeling towards Jews – "anti-Semitism" – particularly so in Germany, and even quite a bit in Britain. Partly this seems to have been jealousy. Jewish people have always tended to stick together and help each other, and to value education, with the result that many of them have become very bright and very successful in business, and also in science. And this, in turn, has made other people resentful. Tola, like Jo, went to the "Free University", where there was no state support and both students and lecturers had to earn their living elsewhere, and this was because the Polish government at that time would usually not allow Jews to attend the official University of Warsaw.

Their friendship deepened, and they wanted to get married, but this wasn't practical until they could afford some sort of a home. Even when Jo had graduated and gone on to work in the Radiological Laboratory (which was a private, voluntary organisation) he wasn't paid a proper salary, and Tola had had to take an office job. And so it was not for another seven years, in 1937, that they were finally able to get married. And, by then, a lot of other things were starting to happen.

Jo's boss, Professor Wertenstein, was getting older, and Jo seemed the obvious person to take over when he retired. But, meanwhile, they wanted to bring in to the lab some of the modern techniques that they needed, and which were already being used in places like Britain and France. And also, it would be a good thing if Jo could have the experience of working in one of the major labs in one of those countries. When Wertenstein was younger, he had done just that, and had spent two years in Cambridge, working alongside that same James Chadwick who had first discovered the neutron (and had been given a Nobel Prize for Physics as a reward). Since then, Chadwick had become Professor of Physics in Liverpool, where he was busy installing a cyclotron, like the one that Glenn Seaborg was going to be working with in California. So Wertenstein and Chadwick arranged that Jo could go and spend a year at the lab in Liverpool, which would give him that much wanted experience of working with the cyclotron.

But, meanwhile, trouble was brewing with the neighbours. At the end of the First World War, in 1918, although Germany had been defeated, popular mood among the victors – France, Britain, USA and their allies – felt that Germany should be made to pay a huge fine for having started the war. In a way this was very unfair, because it wasn't the German people who had decided to go to war but their autocratic ruler, the Kaiser, and his fellow aristocrats. But it happened, and it just piled on the misery for ordinary people in Germany and made them feel bitterly resentful, partly against the old aristocracy but mainly against anyone who seemed to be exploiting their misfortune.

Riding to their rescue, so it seemed, came a gang of politicians wanting German rights for German people, and calling themselves National Socialists, or "Nazis". At the head of this was an Austrian housepainter and wartime corporal by the name of Adolf Hitler. It always helps unscrupulous politicians to be able to make people believe that they have an enemy, even a make-believe one, and Hitler's choice for this was the Jews. This made him popular among a lot of Germans, and soon he was making plans to extend the borders of Germany to win back areas where there had been German-speaking populations. Austria and Czechoslovakia were two of these, but where would it end? There were German-speaking areas of Poland too.

Jo and Tola knew about this, and were very aware that brutal attacks were being made on Jewish people, without anybody being able to stop it. But this was in Germany, not Poland, and, in any case, Britain and France had signed a treaty saying that they would protect Poland if ever it were attacked by Germany. So, they carried on with their plans.

Money – the old, old problem! The Warsaw lab could give Jo a small grant, that would be just enough to support him in Liverpool, but not Tola as well. So, he set off, in July 1939, to get started and see what could be done. There were going to be problems, he knew. For one thing, although he could speak quite a bit of German, Russian and French, as well as Polish of course (and Yiddish), he could hardly speak any English, and even what he had learned wasn't much help in understanding the local, Liverpool 'scouse', dialect. At one stage he was so homesick that he almost gave up and went home, and it was only with Tola's encouragement that he decided to stay. Although he didn't know, it was a decision that probably saved his life.

Eventually, however, things started to look up. James Chadwick was usually a rather shy and unsociable person, but he and Jo got on well from the start and, happily, he was able to find some extra "fellowship" money that would add to Jo's grant and make it possible for Tola to join him. So, in early August Jo was able to write to her to say that he was anyhow going to have to come back to Warsaw for a few days to discuss scientific things with his boss, after which they could travel back to Liverpool together.

Bad luck again! By the time he got back home Tola was in hospital with appendicitis, and wouldn't be fit to travel for another three weeks – she would have to follow Jo to Liverpool later on. So, on a Wednesday evening, 30th August, Jo went on his own to catch the Moscow to Hook-of-Holland train as it passed through Warsaw. He caught the night ferry to Harwich the next day, only to hear the news, when he got off the boat train at London,

Liverpool Street on Friday, that the German army had invaded Poland at dawn, and was advancing on Warsaw. Two days later Britain and France kept their promise to support Poland and declared war on Germany.

Jo's life seemed to be falling apart. He was cut off from his wife and family entirely, knowing that the policy of the Nazi German government was to get rid of the Jews. At that stage it wasn't clear how they would do it, but soon news trickled through that hundreds of thousands of them (together with people like Gypsies, who too weren't considered fit to be part of the new German "Master Race") were being rounded up, taken to internment camps and then gradually starved and gassed to death. One of those camps was near the Polish town of Oswiecim– known to the Germans as Auschwitz. In his desperate attempts to help, Jo asked the famous Danish scientist, Niels Bohr, to try to get Tola across to still-neutral Denmark. Bohr tried his best but, before he could set up an escape, the Germans had invaded Denmark too. So, for the next six years Jo had no news, and could only imagine what was happening to his wife and family.

But life had to go on. When he got back to Liverpool, knowing that his Polish grant had disappeared and hoping that Chadwick could help him with an advance on the fellowship, that was due to start in October, he found that Chadwick was away on holiday in Sweden and unable to get back because of the war. Jo found himself with only 7/6d in the world, and unable to pay his rent. (That would be 35p in present money, but equivalent now to about £20 – still not much to live on!) In desperation he hitch-hiked back to London to ask for help from the Polish embassy, which he found "in complete chaos". Eventually, back in Liverpool, his landlord took pity on him, and let him stay on, and when Chadwick got back he saved the day by appointing Jo as a lecturer in nuclear physics. Some task for someone who couldn't speak English a couple of months earlier, but he got down to it, and started lecturing at the end of November!

So, here he was, in a strange foreign place, cut off from everything and everyone he had known through the previous 30 years of his life, and living in dread for six more years at the thought of what had become of the people that he loved most.

INTO A SECRET WORLD

Perhaps it was a good thing that there wasn't much time to worry. At the same time as learning English and preparing his lectures, Jo had gone back to thinking about his experiments on nuclear fission and whether (awful thought) a nuclear bomb might be possible. Half of him wanted to forget the whole dreadful idea, but the other half was haunted by the thought of what would happen if Hitler and his Nazis had the same idea, made one, and used it to start forcing their "racial cleansing" policies on the rest of us. This could well happen. Although many of their best scientists had been forced to emigrate just to escape this very situation, Germany was still one of the leading scientific countries, and the discoveries of people like Jo had become common knowledge in the scientific world. It was a good bet that, even if they hadn't started already, the Germans would soon be working on this possibility.

So, Jo decided to share his ideas with his new, and rather uncommunicative boss. At first Chadwick just grunted. But he went away and thought about it, and soon came back to ask Jo what experiments he now wanted to do to follow up his ideas, and to give him two assistants to help him (one of these was a Quaker, and a conscientious objector, so Jo felt bad about not being able to tell him the real purpose of the research). And Chadwick also wrote to the government, saying that: "it seems likely that fission could be developed to an explosive process under appropriate conditions". In other words, we can probably make nuclear weapons. And their opinion was soon supported by others. Early in 1940 another similar report came through the government letterbox, this time from two refugee scientists from Hitler's Germany, now working in Birmingham – Rudi Peierls (pronounced "piles") and Otto Frisch.

The spring of 1940 was a desperate time for Britain. The German army, having overrun Poland and made a truce (or so it seemed) with the Russians, had invaded France and forced the British army to retreat across the Channel through Dunkirk, whilst the German air force was making non-stop bombing raids over England. Britain was on its own. It was not until 18 months later, when the USA suffered a surprise attack from Japan, that they joined Britain in war against both Japan and Germany. Whilst all this was going on the UK government decided that a desperate situation called for desperate remedies, in the shape of nuclear weapons.

Chadwick, Jo and the Birmingham group had been very careful whom they talked to, but from now on secrecy had to be absolute. Words like Atomic and Nuclear, were banned and, to foil the spies, the project was only ever referred to by the code name of "Directorate of Tube Alloys".

But the task was huge. No one really knew how large a lump of uranium you would need to make sure that too many neutrons didn't escape from the lump, or get otherwise sidetracked, to ensure that the explosive "chain reaction" actually happened. And there was a complication – natural uranium is a mixture of several "isotopes".

The one that does the fissioning – uranium 235 – is only a small fraction of the mixture and, to make a bomb, or to fuel a nuclear power reactor, you need to get rid of most of the much more plentiful isotope – uranium 238. (In the jargon, this process is called "enrichment", and the stuff that is thrown out is called "depleted uranium" – basically it is uranium 238.) In any case, uranium enrichment is a very complicated and costly process, that was going to be beyond what war-torn Britain could possibly manage. And even then there were doubts. Would a uranium bomb ever work? Might a plutonium bomb be better (if you could ever find a way to make enough plutonium)? Would it be best to make both, in case one didn't work – the belt and braces approach?

Prime minister Winston Churchill wanted the bomb to be British. But he was a realist and, even though America was not in the war, he sent some of his top people over to tell the story to US President Roosevelt and ask if he could help. Then, out of a clear blue morning sky, the Japanese air force made a surprise attack on the American base at Pearl Harbor, in the middle of the Pacific, destroying in a couple of hours a large part of the US navy. This was a real wake-up call. America declared war on Japan, Germany declared war on America, and American interest in nuclear weapons started to take off.

Until then the work in Britain had been absolutely top-secret, with most of it being done in the two fairly small university research groups, in Liverpool and Birmingham, coordinated by a government committee, code-named MAUD, in London. (This name came about because someone misread – and interpreted it as a coded message – a telegram from Nils Bohr in Denmark, who was actually just referring to his children's English nanny, Maud Ray!). But the Americans got into it big time. They made it a top-secret military project, put a general in charge – Lesley Groves – and gave it their own confusing code name, the Manhattan Project, and built a huge laboratory campus for it at a place called Los Alamos, in a remote part of New Mexico, near Santa Fe.

It was to be a US-UK collaboration. Most of the people were American, but there was a strong British group, with James Chadwick in charge. Jo would be an essential member of the group, but Jo was Polish, and the Americans insisted that only Americans and Brits were allowed. But Jo was a patriot – he said he would rather stay out of it than give up his citizenship and, in any case, his plan would be to go straight back to Poland from America as soon as possible after the war. Eventually Chadwick persuaded the Americans to give in and let Jo come to Los Alamos. But, from then on he was a marked man in the files of the American FBI. They were pretty convinced that he was a spy, who would disappear back to Poland and tell all he knew to the Russians, or perhaps the Germans.

Meanwhile the war was going badly for Britain and America. Having threatened to invade Britain, the Germans had overrun Russia, reaching almost to Moscow and Leningrad (St Petersburg), whilst the Japanese had occupied much of East Asia – China, Singapore, Malaysia, Indonesia. But, there was one good thing – messages were coming back from the spies in Germany, who were reporting that the scientists there had done their calculations and come to the conclusion that it would be impossible to make a nuclear bomb.

This was a mistake with huge consequences: if they had got it right, Germany might well have won the war. The people who got it right were Jo and his fellow refugees in Britain. It was all about neutrons: how many of them are produced when a uranium nucleus splits, and how many of those are not wasted but go on to trigger another uranium nucleus to split. If the end result is more than one neutron you get an explosive "chain reaction" – if it is less than one, nothing much happens. (The trick for getting a civilian nuclear power station to work is to arrange that the neutrons from each split of a uranium nucleus go, on average, to trigger a split in just one more nucleus: too few and the thing stops working, but too many is what happened at Chernobyl.) Ironically, if the Nazis hadn't scared away so many of their best Jewish scientists, the calculations might have been done better, and given them the "right" answer!

When Jo arrived in Los Alamos the Chadwicks offered to put him up for a few weeks, until he could find somewhere to stay and, from then on he would often be round for a meal. One evening when he was there the Chadwicks had also invited in the overall boss, General Groves and, as the evening wore on, and they had had a few drinks, conversation got around to the bomb and what it was for. Only then did Jo realise, from what Groves had said, that not only was Germany no longer considered by the Americans and British to be a serious enough problem even to threaten them with nuclear attack, but also that the war in the Pacific was going sufficiently well that Japan was sure to be defeated – it would be a matter of time, but also of course a lot more casualties on both sides. No – the bomb would be used against Japan, partly to try to bring an early end to the war, but with the main reason being to frighten the (supposedly allied) Russians away from doing anything after the war that would threaten American power.

This seemed to Jo to be totally immoral. He had agreed to help develop this terrible new weapon only to try to stop the inhumane Nazi practices of "racial cleansing" – murdering millions of people simply because they

HOW TO MAKE NUKES WORK!

A nuclear explosion happens if a nucleus of an atom of uranium-235 or plutonium-239 splits apart ("fissions"), emits a number of neutrons and, as a result, on average more than one of them goes on to trigger another fission. To discover whether and how this will actually happen turns out to be a very tricky bit of physics indeed, needing careful experiments (some of which Jo did) and complicated theory (some done by his friend Rudi Peierls together with Otto Frisch, both of whom were Jewish refugees from Hitler). For instance, if the lump of uranium is too small, too many neutrons escape from the block before doing their job of triggering a fission. If it is too large – well, it is hideously expensive stuff, and anyhow you may end up with an impossibly heavy bomb. The simple fact is that Jo and his colleagues did their physics right, and the Germans got their's wrong.

Getting the physics right was just the first step – making the thing actually work is still far from easy. What the physics had shown was that you will only get an explosion if the lump of fissile material is heavier than a certain value ("critical mass", in the jargon). For both uranium-235 and plutonium-239 this turns out to be around two kilograms. There is a problem though. If you are too slow and gentle in increasing the mass above the "critical" value (eg in bringing two smaller lumps together), the thing just fizzles – it gets hot, falls apart, and is no longer a critical mass. To do the job properly you have to use a conventional explosive to shoot two or more sub-critical masses together to form – very rapidly – one large critical mass.

That's tricky, but it can be done. At least eight different countries have done it, and the basic know-how is now pretty much common knowledge. Creepy thought – but even worse is the thought, and the reality, of the thousand-time bigger explosion that can be made by the hydrogen bomb (see the box on page 49: "A Million Elephants").

didn't fit in to somebody's idea of a master race. And now the agenda goal posts had been moved – it was now to be all about power politics. Jo decided that he couldn't go on – he would have to resign. In fact this would be a brave thing to do, as Los Alamos was a military operation, and the powers that be didn't talk about resignation – they called it desertion.

And there was another problem. Back in Liverpool, as a friend of a friend, Jo had once met a young American law student, Elspeth Grant. Elspeth had gone back to America and was living in Santa Fe, starting to get seriously deaf, and feeling very lonely. The mutual friend, knowing that Jo was somewhere in the USA, wrote to him and suggested that, if he was ever anywhere near Santa Fe, Elspeth would enjoy a visit. In fact, Santa Fe is not far from Los Alamos, and it was the one place to which the lab staff were sometimes allowed out for a trip; it happened, even, that Jo had started to take flying lessons at a nearby airfield, on his days off. To make personal visits needed official permission, but Jo was given this, and so the two of them were able to meet up. Jo wasn't allowed to breathe a word about where he was based or what he was doing, but they found plenty to talk about, particularly as they were both socialists. Elspeth's deafness meant that she often didn't hear the phone or the doorbell, so Jo rigged up some electronics for her that switched on the lights when the bells rang.

But – the spooks had been watching! When Chadwick asked the administrators to deal with Jo's resignation letter they pulled a long face and showed him a thick dossier of what they said was evidence that Jo was a spy, planning to go back to Poland and tell all to the Russians. Yes, someone had been listening in to Jo and Elspeth's conversations. And, no doubt, Jo's electronic wizardry in Elspeth's home was regarded as very suspicious. Jo's politics were what, in Europe, would make him something like a Social Democrat but, at that time, most Americans thought that socialism was just a form of communism, and so very suspect. But, even in America, having left-wing views wasn't then a criminal offence and, when Jo was confronted with the rest of the evidence, he was easily able to show that it was untrue – it had all been made up!

Even that wasn't the end of the story. Jo had indeed been planning to go straight back home to Poland when the war was over, and he had brought over with him from Liverpool all his personal and family papers and other belongings. So, when he set off back to England after resigning from Los Alamos, he packed these carefully in a box that he had got specially for the purpose. On the way back he stopped off in Washington, DC, where the Chadwicks were now living and, on the following morning, James

Chadwick took him down to catch the boat train to New York, and helped him load the precious box. But, when the train arrived at New York docks the box had disappeared. No one could explain but, almost certainly, the the FBI had suspected it contained the secrets of the bomb, and had spirited it away. Anyhow, Jo never saw it and its contents again – the spooks had taken all the remaining mementos of his family life, even his photos of his family and his wife, Tola.

Back in 1938, before Jo had first arrived in Liverpool, and when Chadwick was first building his famous cyclotron, he had been telling people that some of its uses might be in medicine – treatment of cancer and diagnosis of various diseases. Such ideas had been put on one side during the war but, when Jo got back to Liverpool, late in 1944, although part of his job was to go back to teaching nuclear physics, he wanted his research work to have more definitely humanitarian applications, and so he set about fol-lowing up Chadwick's suggestions about medical uses.

This opens up a new part of the story but, meanwhile, Los Alamos hadn't stopped work.

SHOJI

Shoji Sawada, who was just twelve, hadn't been feeling very well, so his mother had kept him away from school for the day. The other children were OK, so it was just he and his mother who were at home that morning, in their little house, a bit away from the centre of the port of Hiroshima – a city of 350,000 people - roughly the size of Cardiff, Edinburgh or Southampton The rainy, typhoon season had just ended, and now it was a fine, clear day – 6th August 1945 actually – thirty years and a day since Josio and his family had heard the gunfire in Warsaw – and it was starting to feel quite warm even at 8.00am.

The air-raid warning was nothing unusual. American bombers had been coming over most days when the weather was clear like this. There was something curious though. By this time in the war 60% of Japan's other major cities had been 60% destroyed by American bombing but they had hardly touched Hiroshima, even though it was a military base. This time however it was very different. The bomb was nuclear. It exploded at 8.15 and, although it was a good mile away, the house collapsed, trapping Shoji and his mother inside. He managed to work himself free but then discovered that his mother was trapped under a fallen roof beam and, try as he might, he could not free her. On top of this, a firestorm was developing and eventually, with his mother pleading for him to go, he had to leave her and run for the relative safety of the river. His mother was one of 140,000 people who died that day, and there were 70,000 more a few days later, at Nagasaki. The Americans still didn't know which sort of bomb would work best, uranium or plutonium, so they tried one of each.

Later that day, in Liverpool, Jo was listening to the BBC "Home Service" 9.00pm radio news and heard the announcement that a new and enormously powerful "atomic" bomb had been dropped on the Japanese city of Hiroshima. You didn't need to know what Jo did to realise that the world would never be the same again.

A few weeks later the telephone rang. For almost six years, since that fateful day when he caught the train from Warsaw, Jo had been completely cut off from news of his family and friends in Poland. His thoughts had always been going back there – how could they possibly have survived in those terrible conditions, where two in every ten Polish people had died, almost a million in Warsaw alone – many of them Jews who had been sent to the extermination camp at Treblinka? Now, at last, he was going to hear what had happened to them.

The voice on the phone was his sister, Eve. The good news? By a miracle she had survived, together with her husband and daughter, Halina, their brother, Michael and his wife Maria, and their elderly mother. Most of them had been hidden as tenants in a Gentile (non-Jewish) household, whilst their youngest brother, Bronek, had disappeared. And, tragically, Tola had been arrested by the Nazis, sent to an extermination camp, and had never been heard of again. Jo's old boss and friend, Prof Wertenstein, also Jewish, had several lucky escapes whilst he was in hiding from the Nazis, only to be killed by bomb shrapnel whilst he was in Budapest on an errand of mercy for a friend. The end of a nightmare! But Jo made the best of it. He couldn't go back to Poland because the Russians were there again, so he managed to bring the remainder of his family over to Britain, and to start almost a completely new life.

As a scientist, Jo had decided to change track, and try to see how his knowledge of nuclear physics could be put to practical benefit of people – by using it in medicine – trying to prevent disease, and diagnosing and treating it when that failed. This is another bit of his story that we shall come back to. What he also did was to try to persuade people that, with nuclear weapons around, war must no longer be an option.

THE ATOM TRAIN

When the war finally ended, the world was in a mess. Thousands of towns and villages across Europe and Asia had been destroyed; some fifty million people had been killed, many more horribly wounded, and many even of those who had escaped were facing starvation and disease. There was not much to be cheerful about but people needed something to look forward to. Ironically, perhaps, one of the gleams of hope that folks latched on to was the awesome genie that had just been let out of its bottle – nuclear energy.

This was magic beyond most people's understanding, and a lot of weird ideas started to go the rounds. Even usually sensible people started to predict that energy would soon be "too cheap to be worth metering".

Fortunately, not everyone believed in magic. A number of the scientists who understood these things, Jo included, began to realise that only they could properly explain to the rest of us, including politicians, what this genie might do, for better or worse.

A group of these scientists, all of whom had been involved in the war-time nuclear programme, got together early in 1946 to form what they called the Atomic Scientists Association. Its job was to be to let the public know the true facts about the subject, and to help governments find a way to stop it getting out of control. Jo was made its "Executive Vice-Chairman", which was a polite way of saying that he was expected to do a lot of the hard work.

When it came to hard work, Jo was no shirker – quite the opposite. He was soon at it – planning, and trying to raise money for an "Atom Train". This was to be a sort of mini-science museum on wheels. Nowadays it would probably be put in a series of coaches or trailer-trucks but, in 1947, when

IF A BOMB FELL ON LONDON
These effects are based on results obtained from Hiroshima

Illustration, in the Atom Train, of the likely result of a Hiroshima-type bomb dropping on London. Nearly everyone would be killed within half a mile (circle A), with many more deaths and severe burns and injuries further out. Each of the 200 warheads in the present-day British Trident submarine fleet is around five times more powerful than the Hiroshima bomb. But that is dwarfed by the world-wide arsenal of nuclear weapons – equivalent to three tons of conventional explosive for every man, woman and child on our planet.

(A) Nearly every one killed within half a mile.
(B) Severe burns over three quarters of a mile away.
(C) Damage to property and radiation sickness up to two miles.

The Atom Train – open for visitors in 1947.

it started its tour of the country, there weren't many vehicles to spare, there were no motorways, and other roads were in a pretty bad state, so train it was. The Atom Train exhibition was moved around the country, eventually stopping, for about a week at a time, in 26 different stations, and finally going abroad to places like Paris and Copenhagen.

If you boarded the train, you would first of all visit a section called "Fundamental Facts", with sections about atoms and how they behave, radioactivity, atom smashing, and artificial radioactivity. And then, in other coaches, there were exhibits about "Practical Applications": nuclear electricity (see box), using artificial radioisotopes in medicine and industry, and the atomic bomb – how it works, and what one would do if it fell on a city like London. And there would be talks by experts: Jo was one of the regulars.

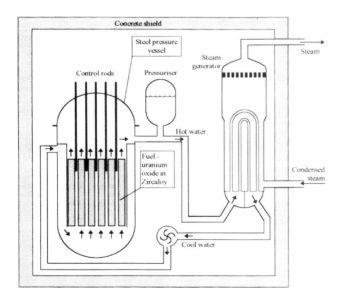

Principle of a common type ("Pressurised Water" or PWR) of modern nuclear power reactor. The uranium fuel is contained in a set of sealed metal cylinders ("rods"), each of which can be lifted up and replaced as the fuel becomes exhausted. Water, under pressure, is pumped through the array of rods, carrying away heat to a steam generator. The water has another function, of slowing down ("moderating") the neutrons produced by fission of the uranium, so making them more efficient at triggering further fission. A set of control rods, which absorb neutrons, is interspersed amongst the fuel. They are automatically raised or lowered to speed up, or slow down the reaction, so keeping it at an optimum, average steady level. In an emergency they drop down, under their own weight, and shut down the reactor.

NUCLEAR ELECTRICY

Electrical power has been part of the lives of many of us for around the past hundred years, although much less than that in a good deal of the developing world. Until nuclear energy became generally available in the 1950s, almost all of this had been produced by heating water over a coal or oil fire, and using the energy in the resulting steam to drive a rotary electric generator by means of a turbine or piston engine. This is actually a very inefficient process: even the best (and, generally, the larger the better) modern turbines struggle to extract much more than 40% of the energy from the burning fuel – most of the rest just goes to waste, and heats up the environment.

Nevertheless, the only practical way that we know for using nuclear energy works the same way – the fission energy given off by the nuclear fuel is used to generate steam. So, the job of a nuclear power reactor is to create heat – you need a lot but (for goodness sake) not too much all at once! There are various designs of nuclear reactor, but they all work on the principle shown in the diagram. The (usually uranium) fuel is enclosed in a large number of packets – usually cylindrical rods – which are interspersed among a number of control rods, made of a material that absorbs neutrons. If the control rods drop right down, too many neutrons are absorbed and the reactor stops working. If they are lifted too far up, the core heats up beyond its safety limit, starts to melt, and may explode. (That is what happened at the Ukrainian Chernobyl reactor in 1986 when the operators switched off the safety system. Modern reactors are designed to make this impossible.) When the reactor is working properly the positions of the control rods are continuously adjusted automatically to keep the core temperature at its optimum value. If something goes wrong, and the temperature starts to rise dangerously, the control rods drop down under their own weight and the reactor shuts down.

For visitors to the exhibition, this would have been quite an experience. This was all about a brand new and exciting bit of science and technology. And also at that time – away from places like the Science Museum in London – there were hardly any science shows of any sort, let alone on a train, so it would have made a great day out for schoolchildren.

For Jo, this, and his other work with the Atomic Scientists Association, turned out to be the start of something much bigger, which would soon take over a large part of the rest of his life. And, for this, chance gave him a powerful ally.

A COOL EARL

Bertrand Russell (Bertie to his friends) had led a curious life. Not long after he was born, in 1872, his parents both died, and he went to live with his grandparents. Grandad – as Lord John Russell – had been Prime Minister (twice), and Queen Victoria had made him Earl Russell – a title that Bertie eventually inherited but which, as he was a socialist and disapproved of titles, he never used. Meanwhile, he was a bright boy, and went to Cambridge University to study maths and philosophy, and before long was writing what became famous textbooks on both subjects. He was left-wing in politics and, during the 1914-18 war, he was an outspoken pacifist. This got him into trouble, and he was eventually put in gaol for six months. He thought this was going to be a waste of time, so used it to write an "Introduction to Mathematical Philosophy"!

So it was, world-famous and a bit of a pain in the backside to the establishment, that he became a leading figure in opposing the development of nuclear weapons. Things came to a head in 1955, when the USA, and then the Soviet Union, started testing a new type of weapon, up to a thousand times as powerful as that used at Hiroshima, the Hydrogen Bomb (see the box "A Million Elephants …").

The Hiroshima bomb had been bad enough but Russell now realised that, with the hydrogen bomb, mankind really was becoming able to pretty well wipe out life on the planet. The politicians didn't seem to realise what they had got themselves into, or anyhow didn't know how to get out of the fix, so he decided to try to get the scientific community to show them the way. His friend, Albert Einstein thought as he did, and offered to help, so that was a good start. Then the BBC asked him to appear on a Panorama TV programme about nuclear weapons. And, to get some scientific expertise, they also asked the Executive Vice-president of the Atomic Scientists Association – Jo Rotblat. Through this chance meeting, Russell had found just

A MILLION ELEPHANTS

Earlier on we talked about a uranium nucleus splitting apart, losing a bit of mass, and releasing a corresponding amount of energy, with a resulting explosion. The uranium atom is very heavy, but something rather similar can happen when two of the very lightest atoms – hydrogen – combine to form an atom of helium. Again, some mass disappears and, to make up for it a lot of energy is released. This is what is going on in the sun – using up energy in that way is what makes the sun so hot, and lets it keep our Earth pleasantly warm. It is a lot of energy, and a lot of mass – something like the mass of a million elephants being used up every second!

Of course, this could only happen at the fantastically high temperatures and pressures that there are in the sun. It would never happen on earth – at least, it wouldn't until there was a nuclear fission bomb.

What people then realised was that, if you wrapped up a fission bomb in a blanket of the right sort of hydrogen (there are several kinds, with different numbers of neutrons in their nucleus, and you need the right mixture), the fission bomb would set off the hydrogen "fusion". And that is what happened – the first time was when the Americans set one off on the small Pacific island of Bikini (which then gave its name to a new fashion in swim suits – but that is another story).

the person he needed to work with him on the project That really got things started.

First of all they wrote a "Manifesto", got Einstein and other world-famous scientists to sign it, and launched it with a lot of high-profile publicity, and a big launch meeting in London, with Jo in the chair. What the Manifesto pleaded for, in a nutshell, was for governments, scientists, and ordinary people to find peaceful ways for settling international arguments – otherwise we shall all blow ourselves up.

Next they wanted to get together the key scientists around the world who were involved in nuclear weapons work and could perhaps combine to persuade their governments to rescue the situation, and advise them how to do it. This was going to be the tricky bit. The Americans and Russians were hardly on speaking terms, and in the American Congress there was a bitter and almost paranoid anti-communist campaign being waged, led by one Senator McCarthy. So, getting the key US and Russian scientists together in one place seemed a hopeless task. They needed money to pay for it, and they needed to find a neutral venue that could be a hideaway from unwanted disturbance and publicity.

They were in luck. Russell received a letter, from a man called Cyrus Eaton, who said he was President of the Chesapeake and Ohio Railroad (his grandfather had been captain of a Canadian Clipper sailing ship). He had seen the Manifesto, and was so impressed by it that he offered to pay for a meeting that could be held at his country home in the remote Canadian fishing village of Pugwash, Nova Scotia – a magical place beside a quiet inlet from the Atlantic, and a good spot, on a lucky day, for seeing hump-backed whales. This was ideal. Canada was neutral, and Pugwash ("Pag-wechk" in Native American, meaning "shallow waters") is such a difficult place to get to that the press, and other intruders, would give up. So they took up the offer. (By the way – the Captain Pugwash of the cartoon, that first appeared in the 1950 first issue of the Eagle children's comic, has never been near the place – goodness knows how he picked up the name).

The Eaton family home at Pugwash, Nova Scotia – venue for the 1957 conference. Since renamed "Thinkers' Lodge" and, in 2008, designated by the Canadian government as a "Place of national historic significance".

The meeting still took a lot of organising and negotiation. Russell was now in his mid-80s, and most of the hard work was done by Jo and another British physicist, Cecil Powell. But eventually, in July 1957, 22 scientists and others from around the world were able to meet. They came to work, but Cyrus Eaton and his wife Anne were kindly hosts, and made sure that there was a warm, family atmosphere for the occasion. Some of the Russians turned up a day early and, on the first evening, although with hardly a word of common language, two of them – Alexandr Kuzin and Sergei Topchiev – teamed up with Cyrus and Anne for a game of croquet. As anyone who has played will know, under British/Canadian rules this can be a surprisingly aggressive game. It turns out that, under Russian rules, it is much more gentle. Interesting!

The scientists came as individuals, expert in their subjects, but not as representatives of any government or organisation. They held complex discussions, in private. What each person said was never made public – only the conclusions of the meeting – so that, when they got home, their governments couldn't punish them for saying the wrong thing. After the meeting they sent a report on their conclusions to the leaders of the big

Joseph Rotblat (wearing glasses) and Cecil Powell arranging details for the original, 1957, conference at Pugwash.

powers. Anne Eaton, who sat through the meetings, taking notes, later wrote to a friend saying: "I must mention the marvellous change of atmosphere here, as though early on these men decided that, although they could not trust each other's governments, they could trust each other"

This set a pattern for the way things would work in the following years, in what became "The Pugwash Conferences on Science and World Affairs", with Jo Rotblat as its key person – for many years Secretary General, and then President. And it really was an historic change in the tide of world affairs: for almost the first time, Russians and westerners were talking to each other in a serious and trusting way about how to stop human kind from destroying itself.

The two youngest participants at Pugwash, Nova Scotia, in 1957 – Joseph Rotblat and Ruth Adams. Ruth was there to help with the organisation, but she too was something of an activist. Her first job, in 1942, had been as "recreation director" in a wartime Oregon shipyard, but she was sacked for a serious misdemeanour: she had organised a dance that was actually interracial! After that first Pugwash meeting she went on to become editor of the Bulletin of the Atomic Scientists.

SOMEONE BLINKED –
FORTUNATELY FOR US THIS TIME

It would be an understatement to say that the US Secretary of Defense, Bob McNamara, was not a happy man. He was on his way from the Pentagon to the White House to tell the President – Kennedy – that US aircraft flying over Cuba, less than 200 miles from Florida, had spotted a number of Soviet long-range missiles, apparently ready to be fitted with nuclear bombs, and threatening the US mainland. What should be his advice to Kennedy? Attack and hope to destroy them all before they could be loaded with warheads? Slim chance! American Presidents don't like to find themselves negotiating with people standing on their doorstep and getting ready to point a gun. But that was the alternative, and the only way out of starting what could well become a war that destroyed the USA, and much of our civilisation as well.

It was touch and go for several days: governments were confronting each other, whilst US and Russian Pugwash scientists – with Jo Rotblat constantly on the phone to Washington and Moscow – were hard at work trying to devise for them a constructive way out. Eventually both sides saw reason, but they might well not have done. This was in 1962. Bob McNamara never forgot the experience, and it later turned out that the US intelligence had got it wrong – the 170 missiles had already been fitted with nuclear warheads. Even if only ten of those had survived an American attack, that would have been enough to wipe out many US cities. Some time later he remarked that "The indefinite combination of nuclear weapons and human fallibility will lead to a nuclear exchange". In less diplomatic language what he was saying was "Don't trust us politicians with things like nuclear weapons – sooner or later we shall muck things up, and there will be a horrible disaster." The "Cuba Crisis" was very nearly that, and probably the most dangerous moment in mankind's history. Something like that must never happen again.

The main way that Pugwash works is to bring together, in "workshops" on a particular subject, expert scientists on that subject from around the world, and ask them to think about the science and forget that they happen to come from Ruritania, or wherever. For example, they might be trying to work out how to check that different countries are not cheating on the treaties that they have agreed to about not building and testing new nuclear (or biological or chemical) weapons. Often it makes sense to include in these groups people with other kinds of experience, and so you can find there generals, admirals, ambassadors or senators. Bob McNamara, who became an active Pugwash member, was one of these, and was able to contribute his first-hand experience of how politicians deal with these things. And it is also useful for Pugwash to have around people like Bob who, even when they are retired from politics, can still get a phone call through to a US or Russian President.

Jo, too, was brilliant at that kind of networking, but not in a conventional way. A lot of people are keen to become part of the celebrity world, but that was not Jo's way. He was always very sure of what he wanted – he liked to "set the agenda" – and there are plenty of politicians and media moguls who want to do that themselves, and not have others making trouble. But Jo became respected by a whole range of more thoughtful and influential people.

OSLO ON THE PHONE

Being an ambassador can be good fun, some of the time at least, but it can also have its boring bits. Michael O'Leary was quite enjoying his new job as the Irish ambassador to Britain but when it came to spending day after day sitting at the back of tedious political party conferences – well, he just wanted to sneak out for a round of golf. This one, though, the 1995 Conservative Party bash, just could be one of those fun occasions. The British and Irish prime ministers – John Major and Albert Reynolds – had been working together for several years, quite successfully it seemed, on bringing an end to the bitter infighting that had been going on for ages in Northern Ireland. The rumour was that the two of them were tipped to share this year's $1 million Nobel Peace Prize for their efforts, and the announcement was due at 11 am today, 13th October. So, when the PA system came to life with the announcement that the start of the 10.30 conference session would be delayed for half an hour, O'Leary jumped from his seat, grabbed his friend the Swedish ambassador, and marched him off to the bar, preparing for a celebration.

At 10.50 the phone did indeed ring – not however at the Blackpool conference centre but 200 miles away in the London office of Pugwash – a rather dingy couple of rooms at the back of an old building opposite the British Museum. It was a Norwegian voice, asking to speak with Professor Rotblat and to tell him that, at 11 o'clock, there would be the public announcement that he and the "Pugwash Conferences" organisation had been jointly awarded the prize. Jo's immediate reaction was to go out for a walk around the block whilst he took in the news. Then, of course, all hell broke loose. The phone wouldn't stop ringing and the press besieged his tiny office, and then went away and mostly, as usual, got the story wrong, either from carelessness or deliberately – it's a sad thing that some journalists will try to smear, as somehow unpatriotic, people like Jo who dare to suggest that the world would be a better place if we turned the other cheek and dumped our lethal weapons in the bin.

But – tomorrow is another day, and some of the journalists would have to wait – he had an even more important, teatime appointment: a birthday party. No Rotblat family party would be complete without the presence of Uncle Josh and his fund of party tricks and games, and after the party, with luck, you might be allowed to go upstairs and play with the console that Uncle Josh had built in his bedroom so that he could control the lights, TV and hi-fi without having to get out of bed.

Meanwhile, the Conservative Party conference carried on without further interruption and excitement.

So it was that, in November, the King of Norway would present Jo with his prize, at a special ceremony in Oslo. Norwegians sometimes have the reputation for being a bit gloomy (their more light-hearted Danish cousins like to say that you need to give a Norwegian at least three beers before he cheers up). But, when it comes to organizing a celebration, they do it in style, and the Nobel party is no exception. As well as their own invitation, the prize-winners are given 100 tickets so that their friends and relations can come and congratulate them, and share the fun – so you end up with a good three days of partying.

ALFRED NOBEL

Alfred Nobel was a Swedish chemist who invented dynamite and went on to make a huge fortune out of explosives and oil. He then decided to use his money on endowing a series of annual prizes – several for the sciences, medicine and literature, and also one for the individual who had "rendered the greatest service to promote international peace". At the time that he made the endowment the Swedish government had been giving the Norwegians a hard time (this was long before Norway had become an oil-rich country). Nobel disapproved of this and, to make a point, decreed that whilst the four other prizes would be awarded in Sweden, the peace prize would be in the gift of Norway.

For Jo this was a wonderful recognition of everything that he had been working on for the past 50-odd years, but it also gave a great boost to what he and his friends were wanting to achieve next in the way of making the world a safer place. Nobel Peace Prize winners find themselves part of a very special and respected club. For Jo and Pugwash this opened up a lot of useful doors – governments that might before have been dismissive of "just another peacenik" suddenly started to listen and get the message. And for Jo in particular it led to a flood of invitations to speak at meetings about nuclear weapons issues, and to meet and discuss with top brass: prime ministers and foreign ministers etc. He did his best by all of these, but couldn't possibly fit everything in; one of his Pugwash colleagues got asked to perform as a substitute invited speaker to the Scientific Society of Andorra!

The official announcement from the Norwegian Nobel committee said that they had decided to give the prize to Rotblat and Pugwash "...for their efforts to diminish the part played by nuclear arms in international politics and, in the longer run, to eliminate such arms." Important stuff, you would think but, in spite of this, a lot of people had never heard of Jo Rotblat, and only knew that Pugwash was a cartoon sea captain. So they couldn't understand why these people were being given one of the world's greatest honours. What had they done to deserve this? Fair question, but the answer goes back to the way that Pugwashites try to operate – aiming to find constructive, scientifically based answers to problems, through thoughtful and well-informed discussions among experts.

There are groups that organize marches and demonstrations, and otherwise stimulate public opinion on issues like this. That is a very important activity – sometimes the only way to get politicians to do something useful – but Pugwash deliberately tries to make its main contribution back-stage.

When government officials meet to negotiate – whether it is about weapons or anything else – there is always confrontation: one country or group of countries is there to try to gain advantage over the other lot. Maybe that is the way things have to go – it is what voters elect governments to do. But Pugwash meetings work in a different way. People are there not because they are British or American, or Russian or whatever, but as expert scientists whose aim is to get at the evidence and work out from that the best way of solving a problem.

The sort of problem that they have been set might be how to work out a foolproof system of checking whether a government is cheating when it has agreed not to produce weapon-grade plutonium. This sort of thing can take a lot of hard work. The experts may have to go home, talk with colleagues, maybe carry out some experiments, and come back together for further meetings. But eventually plans will look good and can be passed on to the official government negotiators who, because the plans are obviously based on the best scientific advice, without being confused by politics and confrontation, will often be happy to agree with each other.

A lot of this sort of thing, partly because it is full of technical detail, does not get much publicity. But sometimes it does, even if a long time later. It was not until 1990, for instance, that it was made public (by the then British government chief scientific advisor), that the first ever international treaty (in 1963) about stopping the testing of nuclear weapons came about considerably thanks to the work of Pugwash. In the same year the President of the Soviet Union, Michael Gorbachov, announced that "Through its activities, due to scientific and moral authority, Pugwash has contributed in an unique way to averting the military danger, and has helped to stop the 'Cold War' and to achieve profound positive changes in the development of the world".

This sounds like rather heavy stuff but, if you remember that the 1945-90 Cold War, and particularly the 1962 Cuba crisis (in which Bob McNamara was so involved), was a potentially catastrophic period for the world, Pugwash is clearly recognized as having made the world a good bit safer. And it has not only been with nuclear weapons problems that the organisation has worked: those in the know have confirmed, for example, that the international agreements that we now have that ban chemical and biological weapons have also been helped to come about through the work of Pugwash – once again with Jo Rotblat very much at the centre of things.

DESERT ISLAND DISC

Celebrity in Britain is a curious business. If you are an ace footballer, or a pop star or TV presenter, that's OK, but if you are just someone who is highly respected around the world for your work and leadership in trying to prevent civilisation from destroying itself, you may need to watch your back! When the news came out of Jo's Nobel Prize – something that has very seldom been given to a Briton, and indeed very seldom to a scientist – neither the Queen nor the Prime Minister offered a word of congratulation. Perhaps Prime Minister Major was still feeling a bit sore that he had lost out to Jo that day. And some of the media could be pretty mealy-mouthed.

Three years later, when a Labour government had come to power, and had arranged for Jo to be given a rather special knighthood ("KCMG" – Knight Commander of the Order of St Michael and St George, but thought by some humourists to mean Kindly Call Me God), one of the right-wing papers ran a headline: "Blair Honours CND". This was a lightly coded way of trying to kill two birds with one stone, and to belittle Jo's work in the process. Right-wingers don't like Labour prime ministers and, although the Campaign for Nuclear Disarmament has been very largely a group of thoughtful, idealistic, and basically patriotic people, it has been a *bête noir* for much of the media. On the day following what all participants could see was its historic and hugely supported inaugural meeting, in 1957, *The* [London] *Times* deliberately ignored it, and that prejudice still lives on. Jo had indeed taken part in the original formation of CND, but had resigned from the committee after a few months in order to concentrate on Pugwash.

Still, he was greatly respected by his fellow scientists and, in 1995, largely for the nuclear physics work that he had done in the 1930s and '40s, he was made a Fellow of the Royal Society – science's equivalent of an Oscar.

Better late than never! But, the real mark of a celebrity is to get an invitation to appear on the BBC radio programme Desert Island Discs. When this arrived, one of his choices was Pete Seeger singing:

Last night I had the strangest dream I've ever had before,
I dreamt the world had all agreed to put an end to war.
I dreamt I saw a mighty room, and the room was filled with men,
And the papers they were signing said they'd never fight again.

He said that he had chosen it because, although the song was written in 1956, he was optimistic that putting an end to war was more in people's minds today than it was fifty years ago. If he was right, a lot of the change was due to his own efforts and leadership.

Jo Rotblat partying with a group of Japanese students

TO GUESS, OR NOT TO GUESS –
THAT IS THE PROBLEM

Back in the summer of 1912 the Isle of Wight holiday makers on Bembridge beach were distinctly puzzled. They were watching a young couple rowing a small boat out to sea. The girl was rowing while the man seemed to be doing a juggling act – trying with one hand to hold up, horizontally, a huge umbrella and, with the other, blowing an old-fashioned tram horn.

Lewis Richardson was trying to work out some physics ideas that had come to him when he heard, a few weeks before, the news of the *Titanic*. This was the wonderful new "unsinkable" passenger liner that had been trying to break a speed record across the Atlantic and, in thick fog, had run into an iceberg and – yes – sunk. As anyone who has climbed a mountain knows, if you shout loudly enough across a steep valley you will often hear an echo, and how soon you hear it depends on how wide is the valley. If you went the right way about it, this could be a way of warning a ship that it was approaching an iceberg – or any other large obstacle. The question which Lewis was trying to puzzle out, and for which he had got his new wife Dorothy to help him, was how best to do the job. He was pointing the horn at a nearby cliff and using the umbrella, just like a modern satellite dish, to concentrate the faint returning echoes.

It took a while to work all this out, and it then started to look quite promising – he had even applied for a patent on the idea. But, by then, it was 1914, and Britain was at war with Germany. Lewis' family were Quakers, and, believing strongly in the Quaker pacifist principles, he decided to drop any more work on this in case it was put to use in warfare, and instead went on to become a brilliant meteorologist – the Met Office even named one of their buildings after him. [see box: "Good echoes …"]

GOOD ECHOES AND BAD ECHOES

Lewis was right to be worried – or anyhow half right. His idea got given the name of "Sonar" – short for Sound Navigation and Ranging – and did indeed get used by navy ships for finding and targeting enemy ships. And the same idea, using radio- instead of sound-signals, so-called radar, has of course become an everyday part of military aircraft and missiles, as well as of ships.
But, on the bright side, thousands of civilian lives are saved every year because ships and aircraft can see where they are going, by means of echo-sounding. And, forty years after Richardson had his idea, people started using a form of echo-sounding – "ultrasound" – to see into the human body. Most people nowadays will have had an ultrasound scan, often the first one when they are still in their mother's womb, and others later, when they are older and at risk of things like cancer and heart disease.

So, the jury is out on whether Lewis Richardson was right to listen to his conscience. He just could not have predicted the balance between the good and the harmful outcomes of his scientific ideas.

Lewis' situation was in a way much more straightforward than Jo's but they were both people – and there have been many others, if not all so famous – who suddenly, and in ways that couldn't have been predicted, found that their scientific work was taking them in a direction that they found morally wrong.

Not everyone, of course, is troubled in this way. It would be unreasonable to point a finger at Ernest Marsden for his student project discovery of the cause of so much trouble – the nucleus. I got to know him quite well in his later life and he never seems to have expressed any concern for the consequences. In fact, to the contrary: in 1943, then a senior New Zealand scientist, he was in Washington and happened to run into Chadwick and his colleague, Mark Oliphant – who were supposed to be there incognito, and under false names – whom he embarrassed by greeting in the hotel lobby with "I can guess why you two nuclear physicists are here", but followed this up by arranging for several New Zealand scientists to join the Manhattan Project.

When the plutonium bomb was exploded over Nagasaki Glen Seaborg might well have felt horror at what had resulted from his discovery, six years earlier, of the new element. But, for him, this had been the right thing to do. And then, five years later, he was at the centre of decisions as to whether the US should develop the hydrogen bomb – the so-called Super. He was quite clear on this, saying that "The only thing worse than our building the bomb would be the Soviets having it when we didn't".

The tradition in the medical profession is for newly qualifying doctors to sign the "Hippocratic Oath", by which they promise always to work in the best interests of their patients. From his own experience, and from seeing colleagues facing similar dilemmas, Jo Rotblat became an outspoken supporter of the idea that newly qualifying scientists should similarly be encouraged to undertake that they would not get involved in research and development work that seemed likely to have warlike applications or lead to bad consequences for humans and the environment. Whether that sort of thing can be brought about is difficult to know. What surely is important though, in science particularly but in all walks of life also, is that we are aware of, and feel responsible for the consequences of the actions and decisions that we take.

SWORDS INTO PLOUGHSHARES – APPLYING PHYSICS IN MEDICINE

This story has been about the decisions that some people can be faced with – and Jo Rotblat is at the centre of it here – when the chances of life and work unexpectedly face them with a moral quandary. For Jo, his quandary was one that had huge implications for the very future of mankind and, from 1945 onwards, much of his life was taken up with trying to find, and to persuade others to accept, a humane solution.

But, there were other important sides to his life, and not least that he became a central and much loved figure for his family members, whom he had been able to bring over to Britain after the war. At the end of the war, although so much had happened, he was only about ten years in to what became a forty-year professional scientific career. Although not so closely connected with it, the "Professor Pugwash" story would not really be complete if we didn't tell something about those remaining thirty years of his scientific work.

Part of the reason that, in 1939, Jo had wanted to come to Liverpool was to work with the "cyclotron" that Chadwick was building there. As we have seen, a cyclotron is just a machine that can spit out things like protons and electrons with such high energies that they can not only travel long distances through solid objects, but can also penetrate into an atomic nucleus and convert it to another, often radioactive, type. Jo and Chadwick were both interested in using it for nuclear physics experiments, but Chadwick was also wondering whether a machine like that could have uses in medicine. A penetrating beam of electrons might be used to treat cancers deep in the body, and artificial radioactivity might be used to trace, remotely, where various drugs and other chemicals were getting to in the body.

These ideas were put aside when the war started. But, when Jo returned from Los Alamos, as well as going back to his main job of teaching nuclear physics, he decided to start some research on how his new knowledge about radiation could be applied in medicine. (see box: "All Sorts of Radiation".)

It will be good to step back a bit here, and try to think what must have been in Jo's mind at this stage. From almost within his own lifetime he had known about the discoveries of x-rays and of radioactivity, first from natural sources such as radium and then man-made. He knew that, for a long time, people had been trying to use x-rays and the radiations from

---

ALL SORTS OF "RADIATION"

Talk about "radiation" can be muddling and, quite often, the people who talk about it can get muddled themselves. The trouble is that the word is used in so many different ways: you can talk about radiation being emitted by anything from a hot fire, through a mobile phone, to radium or a cyclotron. To get a grip on this we need to look back to the "Common Sense Goes Out of the Window" box, and the ideas of atoms working like a set of kitchen shelves, and of radiations being made up of small packets of energy.

Put crudely, we have to think about what these packets of energy can do to the electrons that are sitting on the shelves. The packets that make up heat, visible light, and radio and microwave radiations are all quite small – not energetic enough even to knock electrons up onto higher shelves. X-rays and gamma ray packets however are much more vigorous, and can knock electrons right out of the atom, leaving it as a ("positively charged") "ion". In this form the atom can suddenly become chemically very aggressive – it can damage or alter a molecule that it is part of, or go off and do things to other molecules. And if those molecules are biologically important, particularly if they are the genetically vital DNA, this can have big consequences.

So, there is a very big difference between "ionising radiations" (such as x-rays, gamma rays, alpha- and beta-particles, and the high energy electrons emitted by a cyclotron) and the other, so called, "non-ionizing" radiations (heat, light and radio waves, for example). In medicine it is particularly ionising radiations that are important because, in a word, they can both kill and cure. But, we shall come back to that later.

---

radium to treat various sorts of diseases (from cancer even to conditions like schizophrenia); and he was terribly aware of the deaths and mutilations, some rapid and some long drawn-out, amongst the victims of Hiroshima and Nagasaki. What could he do, with his background and expertise to make something positive of all this? For a scientist, something that seemed in need of much better understanding was just how these, so called "ionising radiations" did their damage. How was it that they could be sometimes lethal, and in other situations curative? Some people were

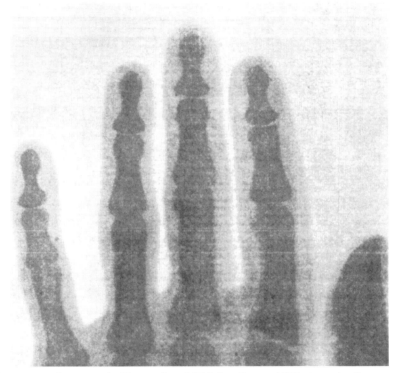

The discovery of x-rays, in December 1896, by Conrad Röntgen in Germany, was the start of a huge revolution in the use of science in medicine. It was followed, in a few months, by Becquerel's discovery of radioactivity, and then by Marie Curie's identification of the two previously unknown, radioactive elements, polonium and radium. The ideas caught on rapidly. This x-ray, of the fingers of a hand, was taken in Liverpool in February 1897 by a Dr Campbell Swinton.

already starting to work on this, in the infant field of "radiobiology". That would be a long-term project, but Jo was also good on practical engineering skills, and keen to get on quickly to do something useful.

A useful starting point for this was that the thyroid gland can often cause trouble – it can get too large, or too small, or develop cancer – and it also has a peculiar liking for iodine, which was one of the elements that you can produce in radioactive form with a cyclotron. So, he got to work on this with a medical colleague at Liverpool and, before long, was able to give a patient a dose of radioactive iodine and then, using a Geiger counter, check whether the iodine had got into the right parts of the gland. This could tell you whether it was diseased, perhaps by cancer, and was a first, and the start of what in a modern hospital is called Nuclear Medicine.

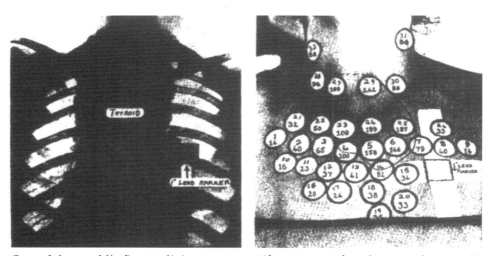

One of the world's first radioisotope scans (forerunner of modern Nuclear Medicine), made in 1948 by Jo Rotblat and his clinical colleague, Dr Ansell. The scan is on the right (with the corresponding x-ray on the left) and was recorded point-by-point over the patient's neck. Each little white circle shows where a measurement was made; the top number in each circle shows the order in which the measurements were made, and the bottom number the Geiger counter reading at that point from radioactive iodine. The dotted line shows the indicated location of the patient's thyroid.

Then a new job came up. The Professor of Physics at St Bartholomew's (Bart's) Hospital in London was retiring and they needed someone to come and teach physics to their medical students. Jo applied for the job, and got it – at least, he thought he had. He was due to start in October 1949 but, just before that, he was told that there was a problem – don't worry, we'll pay your salary, but just stay in Liverpool until we have sorted it out. Jo had been appointed professor by the University of London, but some people at Bart's in those days were a bit stuffy and apparently a few of them had objected to having such a "foreigner" in a senior hospital job. Eventually the university told them that they could either have Jo or nothing, so they gave in. Not a very friendly welcome, but he soon got over it and was hard at work teaching, and starting new research.

Jo had for long been an enthusiast for cyclotrons and part of the attraction for him of the Bart's job was that the hospital had just decided to buy what in some ways was going to be an even better machine for medical work, particularly for treating cancers deep in the body – a "linear accelerator". This was then a new invention, and Bart's was one of the first hospitals in the world to have one, although now it is standard equipment for almost any hospital that specialises in cancer treatment. In fact, when the Bart's machine was delivered, the hospital hadn't yet got space for it, and it was set up in Jo's physics department, so that it could be calibrated and the bugs got out of it.

In the end it never worked very well as a hospital machine, but it was good enough for Jo to follow up what he had been worrying about ever since Hiroshima – what does radiation do to the human body? Why did so many people die days and weeks after the bomb had been dropped? How did many others eventually develop cancer, or have malformed children? And just how can that same radiation be best used to destroy cancers once they have started to grow? Questions like this became the central theme of his department's research for the next 25 years, and it was because of his expertise in this study of "radiobiology" that he was selected for the BBC programme on which he first met Bertrand Russell – the fateful meeting that led to the foundation of Pugwash. (See box: "Kill and Cure – How does Radiation do it?")

KILL AND CURE – HOW DOES RADIATION DO IT?

At Hiroshima and Nagasaki over 100,000 people died from the effects of ionising radiation; and yet now, every year around the world, some ten million cancer patients are treated with a near-lethal dose of it. A paradox – until you realise that what the radiation is doing is screwing up the way that living cells reproduce themselves. It all goes back to the "ionised" atoms that have been stripped of an electron, turning them into chemically voracious agents (see the previous box). Sometimes the cells affected by these agents are stopped from being able to divide, and so to produce healthy offspring; other cells can be changed into a slightly different variety, that cannot respond to messages from their surroundings telling them to stop reproducing. A similar thing happens when eggs or sperm are hit by radiation, and the changes in these cells are of a kind ("mutation") that are passed on to any children, sometimes resulting in abnormalities.

In a healthy body, cells get worn out, or lost, and their way of coping with this is to divide in half and start again. For instance, your red blood cells last for about three months before they wear out and have to be replaced. There is one of the body's many control mechanisms at work that keep red blood cell count just right: too few, and you get short of oxygen; too many and the blood gets too thick to flow properly. (If you go backpacking to Nepal the control mechanism will take a week or so to add the extra blood cells you need for easy breathing.)

The people of Hiroshima were hit with a triple whammy. Many were burned to death, either by the direct effect of the intense (non-ionizing) heat radiation, or by having their houses knocked down and burnt around them (remember Shoji's mother). The ionising radiation did two different sorts of damage. People near the centre of the explosion received enough radiation to stop most of their cells reproducing. The cells that make up the lining of the intestine turned out to be a critical weak link here – they get a lot of everyday wear and tear but are usually replaced every two or three weeks. But, when the replacement mechanism was knocked out, the intestine started to lose its lining, making it leaky and allowing lethal infections to seep in to the body, causing death within a month. Many people living further away still had a lot of damage to their cells, of the sort that changed them into a variety that couldn't stop reproducing – which is how cancer happens.

Treating cancer with this sort of radiation relies on the same bit of science. Cancers are abnormal tissues that have escaped the control mechanism designed to stop them over-growing. So, treating them with radiation is an emergency way of stopping this promiscuous reproduction. It is not easy to get it right though: too much radiation in the wrong place and you injure the patient; too little, and a lot of the rogue cells escape, and start growing again.

For all scientists it is a vital part of their work to make public the results of their research, and they like to do this by publishing it in a scientific journal that is recognised around the world as one that sets and maintains high standards. It is therefore a great mark of professional recognition to be chosen to be editor of such a journal that covers your particular scientific field. This recognition came to Jo soon after he came to work at Bart's Medical School: he was appointed editor of what was then a rather new and struggling journal – *Physics in Medicine and Biology* – but quite soon built it up to becoming very successful, and well known around the world, as indeed it still continues to be.

AFTERWORD – JO AND HIS FAMILY

Although I had known and worked with Jo for about half of his long and varied life, and we had become good friends, when it came to writing about his family and personal life, I found I needed help. This came, very kindly, from his niece, Halina Sand, Eve's daughter. It makes a complex tale and, whilst we both wanted it to be told in some detail, I decided not to introduce too many distractions and digressions into the main part of the story, but to keep them for this section of the book.

Joseph Rotblat was born into a family that was part of a Jewish community that had been living in Poland for centuries, but mostly as a separate, ghettoised group, despised by some and often persecuted by the Christian Polish majority. This racial discrimination was reflected in the university system. In many faculties, such as medicine, Jews were totally excluded whilst in others, perhaps Physics, just a few could be admitted if they could afford it (which Joseph's family couldn't, when the time came). Not surprisingly, this sort of discrimination provoked a lot of bitterness. Joseph's mother would have winced if her children had really referred, in her presence, to "St Casimir's Day": she had a horror of anything that could be considered Christian.

Joseph's sister, Eve, remembered their father as a "patriarch"; the kindest of men, who never struck a child, nor raised his voice to one, but who had *gravitas*: his mere presence exercised absolute authority, and no-one ever sat in his chair in his absence!

Name-giving in the Warsaw Jewish community seems to have been complicated. Joseph's parents and their generation spoke Yiddish at home, and often only rather broken Polish outside, although their children would speak fluent Polish, becoming the first generation to reject the ghettoised existence. Joseph's father's proper (Jewish) name was Zelman, but this became Zygmunt in Polish. Some of the children, similarly, had both Jewish and Polish names; Ewa translated to Eve, for example. Their brother Mordecai (as in the Old Testament Book of Esther), or Motek at home, didn't have a Polish equivalent name until, during the war, the family was in hiding and their Gentile landlord thought the Jewish names too weird, and renamed him Michael (which stuck for life).

Michael and his wife, Maria, together with his mother, managed to get to England soon after the war, coming to live with Jo in Liverpool, where their daughter Frances was born, and then moving with him to London. Unlike his brothers, Michael was not intellectually minded, but he could turn his hand to anything and is remembered with great fondness by his niece. For much of Jo's London life, in addition to running her own family, Maria became devoted to looking after his needs.

Their youngest brother, Bronisław (pronounced Broniswav) was Bronek to his family and friends. He too studied at the Free University, becoming an industrial chemist. At the outbreak of war he was working in a distillery close to the Russian border. He was captured by the Germans and ordered to be shot, but was rescued in the nick of time by a Russian partisan group, whom he then joined. For the next 15 years he was trapped in Russia, and the family knew nothing of him, and assumed that he was dead; but he then managed to get himself repatriated to Poland and then, with Joseph's help, he and his wife got to Britain. He and Joseph had a lot in common and, after his death, and when Maria could no longer cope, his widow, another Halina, known as Hala, came to live opposite Joseph and was his devoted housekeeper for the last ten years of his life.

News of Joseph's wife, Tola, also only emerged after the war. She had joined her parents at their home in Lublin, having refused Jo's family's plea to throw in her lot with them in Warsaw. Her father died a natural death but, soon after, Tola and her mother were arrested and were sent to their deaths in the Nazi extermination camp at Majdanek. Felix Lachman, Jo's college friend, through whom he first met Tola, survived the war, coming to live in England, where he and his wife became regular guests at Jo's family parties.

FURTHER WORD – A PERSONAL NOTE

Science is all about people, and how their wonderful gift of curiosity sometimes leads them into extraordinary and unexpected places. And it is a very social activity – scientists learn from each other, and inspire each other, gradually building up knowledge and ideas as a collaborative effort. Jo Rotblat was a part of this, and although this story is his, it only makes sense when told alongside glimpses of the sort of people alongside whom his knowledge and ideas evolved. There are many to choose from and I have mainly picked examples from people whom I have known in some way.

My first serious meeting with Jo was in 1960, when I found myself on the wrong side of the table at a PhD oral exam. Fortunately, that day, we parted on good terms, and the relationship gradually improved from then on. We were both physicists, working in two different London hospitals, and both of us members of London University, so our paths crossed fairly frequently. For part of that time my boss was Jack Boag, who was an old friend, and some time colleague of Jo's, and it was through Jack that, in about 1992, I became a member of the British Pugwash Group, of which Jo was then the leading member. I was quite soon asked to take over from Jack as its secretary, so finding myself working closely with Jo, and taking part in a number of international Pugwash conferences and workshops. A particular highlight was to have been invited to attend, with my wife Susan, as Jo's guests, the 1995 Nobel Peace Prize award, in Oslo, jointly to Jo and Pugwash Conferences.

Jo was always keen to get his ideas – on attaining a peaceful world, and at least ridding it of terrible weapons – to a wider, and particularly younger, audience. Thus when, soon after his death in 2005, two books of memoirs on his life were published – a total of some 700 pages, written by over sixty contributors – it seemed to some of us that there was material there that would interest a less technical, and perhaps sometimes younger, readership. Writing this book has been an attempt to put that together.

Scientists are sometimes portrayed as cartoon characters – Boffins – who beaver away in back rooms and never talk to anybody. Perhaps there are some such, but I have seldom met one, and I can hardly think of anyone such whose work has made the world a very different, let alone better place. It is the nature of science that people interact and stimulate each other, sometimes working very closely together, as Jo did with Chadwick, and sometimes almost unconsciously, because in the end the different branches of science all fit together, and people working on one problem end up providing clues for others doing something that might have seemed totally unconnected.

So it was with Jo, and I have brought in to Jo's story a number of characters – Ernest Marsden, Glenn Seaborg, Shoji Sawada, Lewis Richardson and others – whose lives have in some ways impinged on, or paralleld, his.

As a young research student, I was given the job of looking after Marsden, when he came to spend six months in our lab, having just retired from being senior scientific advisor to the New Zealand government. He came to Britain equipped with a Fellowship of the Royal Society (the Oscar of the scientific world), a knighthood and, his first wife having just died, a charming new wife whom he had met as the travel agent who booked his boat trip! We were then doing work on the natural radioactive isotopes in the human body that emitted the alpha particles that he had used for his student project fifty years previously.

Shoji first told me his story when, in 1995, the 50th anniversary of the bomb, we found ourselves at the same table at breakfast in the coffee shop of an Hiroshima hotel, where we had both just arrived for a Pugwash conference. After the bombing he had been able to go to college, and become a professional physicist. He had come to the conference to tell the story of his experiences.

I learned quite a bit about Seaborg when I was asked to review his autobiography, and a friend of ours is great nephew of Richardson, who was also the originator of the concept behind much of my own scientific work: the use of acoustic echo techniques in cancer diagnosis.

Working on Pugwash projects brought me alongside both Bob McNamara and Rudi Peierls, and I have sat at the feet of both Bertrand Russell and Niels Bohr to hear them lecture: Russell an elfin, nineteenth century character; and Bohr almost incomprehensible through the thickness of his Danish accent.

And I can still remember being called in from the garden, on Sunday 3rd September, 1939 (not August 1915!) to hear prime minister Chamberlain announce that we were at war with Germany, and also, on 6th August 1945, hearing the BBC report of the Hiroshima bomb, and immediately realising that the world would never be the same again.

All this is to say – what should be obvious – that I have not tried to tell the full story of Jo's professional and public life in all its detail. I have tried, as far as possible, to stick to the important facts but have brought in some walk-on characters who were part of the interactive world in which he lived. Of the many to choose from, I have selected just a few, some of whom I too happen to have worked with or known about.

POSTSCRIPT:
A mystery solved – Captain Pugwash Ahoy!

As this book was going to press, I received the following message from John Cary – animation artist who created some of the Captain Pugwash TV programmes, and close friend of John Ryan, originator of the 1950s' cartoon: "John ….had come up with the idea of a pirate captain. For a name he had toyed with variations of 'Bigbash', Bigwash', 'Bishbash', etc, until he hit upon 'Pugwash'. He was not aware of the village, or the conference, until he read about it in the papers, at which point he created a beautifully worked scroll with a message of congratulation, as if from Captain Pugwash, wishing them well with their deliberations".

SOURCES AND FURTHER READING

There is a great deal of material to be found on the web about Jo and his life, eg under "Joseph Rotblat" and "Pugwash Conferences". Some of the following will be found there, others probably not.

Joseph Rotblat: Visionary for Peace; edited by R Braun et al, Wiley-VCH, 2007.

War and Peace: the Life and Work of Sir Joseph Rotblat; edited by P Rowlands and V Attwood, University of Liverpool, 2006.

Sir Ernest Marsden: 80th Birthday Book; (no named editor), A H & A W Reed, Wellington, NZ, 1969.

Adventures in the Atomic Age: From Watts to Washington; Glenn T Seaborg with Eric Seaborg, Farrar, Strauss & Giroux, New York, 2001.

Prophet or Professor? The Life and Work of Lewis Fry Richardson; O M Ashford, Adam Hilger, 1985.

Bertrand Russell: A Biography; Caroline Moorhead, Sinclair-Stevenson, 1992.

The Ash Garden; Dennis Bock, Harper Perennial Canada (2001). Pure fiction – a story based on the supposed life of a Joseph Rotblat look-alike (of whom the author tells me he had never heard).

INDEX